GOD
IS
ALWAYS
HIRING

GOD IS ALWAYS HIRING

50 Lessons for Finding Fulfilling Work

REGINA BRETT

GC

GRAND CENTRAL
PUBLISHING

NEW YORK   BOSTON

Grand Central Publishing
Hachette Book Group
1290 Avenue of the Americas
New York, NY 10104

www.HachetteBookGroup.com

Printed in the United States of America

RRD-C

First Edition: April 2015
10 9 8 7 6 5 4 3 2 1

Grand Central Publishing is a division of Hachette Book Group, Inc.
The Grand Central Publishing name and logo is a trademark of Hachette Book Group, Inc.

The Hachette Speakers Bureau provides a wide range of authors for speaking events. To find out more, go to www.hachettespeakersbureau.com or call (866) 376-6591.

The publisher is not responsible for websites (or their content) that are not owned by the publisher.

Library of Congress Cataloging-in-Publication Data has been applied for.

ISBN 978-1-4555-5636-6

To Bruce—
My husband, my cheerleader, my forever boyfriend

Contents

Introduction 1

1. When you don't get what you want, you get something better—experience. *3*

2. Everything changes when you change. *8*

3. Burying your talents won't make them grow. *14*

4. What they call you is up to them. What you answer to is up to you. *19*

5. In this drama of life, there are no small parts. *24*

6. Give others a second chance to make a first impression. *29*

Contents

7. Every job is as magical as you make it. *34*

8. There's a time for everything but not always at the same time. *38*

9. Only you can determine your worth. *45*

10. Even the mistakes belong. *51*

11. If you're going to doubt anything, doubt your doubts. *55*

12. Sometimes the job you want is the job you already have. *59*

13. Most of the time, the only person in your way is you. *65*

14. God is still speaking. *70*

15. Make gentle the life of this world. *75*

16. Sometimes your mission is revealed moment by moment. *80*

17. When things fall apart, they could actually be falling into place. *85*

18. When you fail, fail forward. *91*

19. Choice, not just chance, determines your destiny. *97*

Contents

20. It's not about what you can do, but what God can do through you. *102*

21. Instead of trying to be the best in the world, be the best *for* the world. *108*

22. If you can help someone, do; if you can hurt someone, don't. *113*

23. It's important to know both your superpower and your kryptonite. *119*

24. God completes our work. *124*

25. Not everything that counts can be counted. *129*

26. Don't confuse your work with your worth. *135*

27. Clear the path for the person who comes after you. *141*

28. Just because someone isn't on your path doesn't mean they're lost. *147*

29. Expand your comfort zone to make others more comfortable. *152*

30. There's no whining on the yacht. *157*

31. No one can drain you without your permission. *161*

Contents

32. There's more to life than making it go faster. *168*

33. Instead of planning a better life, start living one. *172*

34. The world needs people who are fully alive. *177*

35. The best use of your life is to love. *182*

36. To find out who you are, let go of who you aren't. *188*

37. Align yourself first, then take action. *194*

38. The most important boss to answer to is the small, still voice within. *200*

39. Power is an inside job. *205*

40. It's up to you to launch your life. *210*

41. Things don't happen to you; they happen for you and for others. *216*

42. Don't die with your music in you. *222*

43. Nothing you want is upstream, so stop struggling. *227*

44. Create a pocket of greatness right where you are. *232*

45. Even when you feel invisible, your work isn't. *237*

Contents

46. You make a living by what you get; you make a life by what you give. *242*

47. Be somebody's hero. *249*

48. For networking to work, we all have to be the net. *254*

49. If you don't want regrets at the end of your life, have no regrets at the end of each day. *260*

50. Find your grail. Be who God meant you to be, and you will set the world on fire. *265*

Acknowledgments 271

About the Author 274

GOD
IS
ALWAYS
HIRING

Introduction

In the past five years, I've had the pleasure of speaking in front of thousands of people at countless appearances and book signings. The question I'm most often asked is: "What's your next book going to be about?"

When I tell audiences I want to write a book to help people find more meaning and passion at work and in their lives, they cheer and want to read *that* book right now.

So here it is.

God Is Always Hiring is a collection of inspirational essays, stories, and columns with lessons to help people look at their work and their lives in a new light.

It's for people who no longer love the work they do.

It's for people who love their work but want to find more meaning outside of work, in the rest of their lives.

It's for people who are unemployed, underemployed, or unhappily employed.

It's for people who have been derailed, temporarily or permanently.

It's for people who are just graduating into the world of work and want to know what to write on that clean slate.

It's for people who have retired or can no longer work who want to live a more meaningful life.

It's for people who love the work they do so much, they want to inspire others to find their unique passion in life.

It's for people like me who once felt lost in life and wandered aimlessly along a broken road that ultimately led straight to the perfect place in life. I believe there is a perfect place for each of us. Our job is to find it. Or to relax and let it find us.

I wrote this book to help you find the work you love and create a life you love around your work. Regardless of who your boss is, what your income is, or what the economy is doing, you have the power to expand, enrich, and deepen your own life and the lives of others.

These lessons come from my life experience as a single parent for 18 years, from my perspective as a breast cancer survivor, and from the lives of others I've met at various jobs and in my 29 years as a journalist. My hope is that each lesson helps you jump out of bed in the morning, enjoy a lunchtime boost, feel tucked in at night, or simply gives your life a jolt or a bit of sparkle to make your work and your life matter.

When you don't get what you want, you get something better—experience.

Most résumés don't show the broken road life takes you on or the names people called you along the way. We pretty up our résumés, rename the jobs we had, leave out the parts we wish we could have skipped.

My résumé used to change every six months. Early on in my life, that's about how long I lasted at most jobs. Six months. I was a work in progress. I just wasn't making much progress.

The song "Take This Job and Shove It" was the sound track to my life. I could relate to that other country song, "It's Five O'clock Somewhere," which describes a time when the boss pushes you over the limit and you'd like to call him something, but you'd better just call it a day. One day I didn't. I stormed out of the restaurant and quit my waitressing job. I didn't even stop on my way out to empty the tip jar.

Some people climb the ladder of success. I walked under it. For years I didn't seem to have much luck, and the luck I had seemed bad. My first boss was a real bitch. Seriously. She was a poodle named Mam'selle who lived next door. My first paying job was to walk the neighbor's dog. Mam'selle wore bright red nail polish and a bow. After a long walk with that fluffy ball of white, she finally did her business and I brought her home. The owner lifted up the poodle's puffy Q-tip of a tail.

"You...didn't...wipe her?!" she gasped.

I swear Mam'selle gave me an evil grin. I didn't last long at that job. I thought I was hired to be a dog walker, not a dog wiper.

My next job was to be a personal assistant at a dinner theater that had just opened. The boss ran me ragged cleaning dressing rooms and bathrooms. I was in high school and didn't get home until after midnight. My parents fired me from that job. Then I upgraded to being a cashier at Clark's Pharmacy, where I spent most of my time dusting vitamins and trying to look busy and not get caught sneaking candy bars. Then on to waitressing at Widener's Family Restaurant, where people left me pennies for tips in a puddle of ketchup.

I moved on to the local hospital, where I wore a pink uniform and a hairnet. I stood in white shoes for hours putting prune whip for sick patients on trays on a long conveyor belt. The employee ID card I carried gave me the lovely title Kitchen Help. The title I put on my résumé read Dietary Assistant. I still have the hairnet and ID badge glued to my scrapbook to remind me of those days working 6 a.m. to 3 p.m. in the dish room hosing down trays and dishes that sick people threw up and bled on. I'm not sure we even wore protective gloves back then.

For a while I worked as a secretary. That was BC—before computers. Back then, you were lucky if you were issued an IBM Selectric with eraser tape. I got ink-stained hands from arm-wrestling carbon paper. I used to be a Wite-Out wiz. I'm surprised my boss didn't find me passed out over the keyboard from the fumes. I hated the job. One day it took me all morning to type a three-page letter, only to have my boss hand it back to me after he drew huge circles of red ink around typos that Wite-Out would have covered. I had to retype the whole thing.

It took me many jobs to realize I wanted something more than a job. A job is where you work so you can pay the bills. A job is a place where you're penalized if you're five minutes late even if you stopped to help a stranded motorist. A job is a place where you call in sick so you have time to look for a better job. It might be stable and safe, but it's boring. You do what's expected and you go home. You call in sick every time you rack up enough sick pay because you're sick of the place.

A job is for making a living. A career is for making a life. A job is a paycheck. A career is a bigger paycheck. A career requires education, training, and taking risks. So I set out to get a career. I changed my college major six times, from biology to botany to conservation to English to public relations to journalism. Kent State University had mercy on me and applied its academic forgiveness policy to my GPA after I flunked chemistry and got Ds in zoology and child psychology. It took me 12 years to get a 4-year degree because I took time off to work and raise a child. I started college in 1974 and didn't graduate until 1986, when I was 30. Then it was time to take that degree in journalism and find my mission in life.

I used to think only people like Mother Teresa and Gandhi had a mission in life. We all have one. How do you find it? You listen to your life.

All those dead-end jobs? There's no such thing. In God's economy, nothing is ever wasted. The dots all connect in time. As a kid, I used to love those coloring books with the connect-the-dot pictures. Each dot had a number, which made it easier to discover the final picture. In real life, the dots aren't numbered.

My zigzag route looked like a broken road for the longest time, until one day all the dots connected. As one friend told me, God writes straight with crooked lines. I love that Rascal Flatts song lyric that says, "God blessed the broken road that led me straight to you." God did bless my broken road. I was never lost. God always knew right where I was.

All those jobs I used to call meaningless and mindless vastly enriched me. I just couldn't see it at the time. That meager $200-a-week paycheck blinded me to the wealth of experience I was getting.

Jobs that some people call menial gave my life meaning. My tour of duty as a waitress taught me compassion for the blind man who came in every Wednesday for liver and onions and knocked people out of the way with his white cane as he shouted out his order.

The job at the funeral home taught me how to comfort people in grief so I could have compassion years later as a reporter when I interviewed the father whose son was shot riding home on his bicycle. Working as an emergency medical technician, straddling that place where life meets death, taught me more about deadlines than any editor in a newsroom could.

Every secretarial job taught me how to type better and faster. My job as an alcoholism counselor taught me how to tell when people I interviewed were lying, like the client who served time in prison but didn't think killing a man while he was drunk had anything to do with having a drinking problem.

Working as a clerk in traffic court writing ticket information in court dockets helped me know where to find court records when I did an investigation into how a man with 32 DUIs kept getting his license back before he killed two college students with his car.

My job as a legal secretary typing long legal briefs helped me understand the court system, so when I wrote about an innocent man on death row, it led to a law being changed in Ohio so prosecutors could no longer hide evidence. After 20 years in prison, that man is now free.

They say, "Life is what happens when you're making other plans." So does your résumé. It takes on a life of its own if you let it. Some people try to map out their paths and plan every step, but in reality, life hands you something better. A dead end is really a detour to a new route you hadn't planned on taking. Every experience enhances your life now or later. Without my knowing it, each job I tolerated prepared me to do the work I now celebrate.

You can't always see the growth when your life is taking root. If you're one of those people who feel lost in life, take heart. Being lost could lead you to the very place life planned on taking you anyway.

Everything changes when you change.

It was either the key to the future or a deal with the devil. I wasn't sure which, so I wasn't sure what to do with the document in my hand.

At 22, I had become a parasite on my parents. I had no job and no prospects of one. As an unwed mother, I couldn't support myself or my new baby. It wasn't fair to live rent-free with my parents forever. Plus I felt like I was wearing an invisible scarlet *A*. It stood for Awful. Awful daughter. Awful sister. Awful mother.

Getting help from my daughter's father was out of the question. I wrote him off before she was born. I told him I didn't want to marry him, so I couldn't go to him now. What if he took her away? What if he told the courts he could give her a better life than I could?

I had dropped out of college after I got pregnant. I quit my job working as an emergency medical technician when I was four months pregnant. Back then, the local funeral homes ran the ambulance services. In addition to saving lives, I had to make death calls at hospitals, nursing homes, and residences. Picking up dead bodies wasn't glamorous work, but it paid the bills, and, as we used to joke, no one complained. But after I got pregnant, I couldn't afford to hurt my back or my baby lifting people who weighed more than 300 pounds. The funeral home didn't want to pay for more than two attendants on duty, so I quit.

I didn't know where to get my next job. How could I leave my baby all day to work? She had only one parent. If I was gone all day, it would be like she didn't have any. Factory jobs were out. There was no flexibility. Working 7 a.m. to 3 p.m. meant she'd wake every day to spend the day with someone else. The 3 p.m. to 11 p.m. shift meant I'd never get to tuck her in. The 11 p.m. to 7 a.m. shift meant she'd never get to sleep at home.

I applied for jobs, but I had few skills. I couldn't even type. Buying a car seemed impossible, so I borrowed my dad's. When you're a single parent, it's hard to dream alone. You need money to go with dreams. Other than having a baby, my life was bankrupt. That's how I ended up with those papers in my hand.

Officially the document was called an application for Aid to Dependent Children. But in my small town, we called it what it was: welfare. I debated what to do with the 32-page form. Going on welfare seemed so much easier than finding a job and day care that wouldn't eat up every dollar. With welfare, I would also get medical care for me and my daughter. It seemed like the responsible thing to do.

But every time I tried to sign my name to the forms, I couldn't. I would have to legally name her dad as the father so they could go after him for child support. I didn't even name him on her birth certificate. In the end, the real reason I didn't sign the form was this: I was afraid if I ever got on welfare, I'd never get off. Welfare is a tricky benefit. It starts out as a lifeline to freedom that can become a rope that keeps you in bondage. Any time you want to earn any extra money by working, you risk losing all your benefits and health care.

It's hard to find work in a small town when you don't have a car. There's no bus or subway, no public transportation. Just personal transportation. You're limited by how far your two feet can carry you to and from work. The funeral home a mile away was walkable. I didn't want to go back to picking up bodies, but they offered me a job doing office work, so I took it.

I fell in love there. Not with the job, but with the boss. Bad idea, but desperation does funny things to you. It can make a raging alcoholic look like Prince Charming. I fell in love with everything he had: success, money, and happiness. He owned a gorgeous home. He wore suits to work. He ate out at restaurants. So he drank a little. Okay, a lot. Blackouts, driving drunk, missing work.

In the months we dated, I made it my job to save him. If I could save him, I could have my happily-ever-after. I would make him want me so much he wouldn't want to drink. We spent hours in deep conversations that he never remembered. We made plans to meet at 8 p.m. and he would call at 10 p.m. from a bar saying he was on his way. When the bars closed at 2 a.m. he would finally show up too drunk to stand and then pass out on the couch.

Finally, my friends who knew about Al-Anon told me I needed to detach with love, to stop counting the number of drinks he had, and to stop counting on him to change. There was no future with him, but there was no future without him. I loved his home. It had a breakfast nook and a big porch and bedrooms for all the imaginary kids I fantasized we would one day have. Before I could leave la-la land, though, he left me.

By then my daughter was a toddler. She was growing up even if I wasn't. I finally saved enough money to move out of my parents' house and into an apartment two blocks away from them. It was scary to depend on that meager paycheck for the $210 rent and the utilities. Plus, it was my first time on my own. I had never gone away to college, never lived in a dorm, never had to manage my own life.

All the pieces of my life that had shattered when I became pregnant were starting to fall into place. Every six months I moved to a better-paying job. I found new female friends, including a woman who took me on a retreat to help me get my life on track. There a priest advised me to change the pattern I had with men. I never got around to it. Two weeks later, I was in love.

David was six foot something, drove a Mazda RX-7, wore designer clothes, and didn't drink. He was a teenager emotionally, but so was I. One day he showed up with a souped-up Corvette and I drove 130 mph down the highway. We took off for weekends on a whim, with my mom stuck watching my daughter.

David sent me flowers, bought me clothes, and took me on vacations. He had money to blow all the time. When he blew it on me it was fine; when he blew it elsewhere, I got angry. I didn't know that it wasn't his money; it was his parents'. After one vacation, the credit card company sent someone to his house to cut up the credit cards.

David was going to college for free on government aid. He was skipping classes to play poker and ride his motorcycle. I worked long hours at jobs that paid little. He drove a fancy car while I drove a used bright orange Ford Fiesta I bought for $2,300, every single dollar of which I had saved. It was held together with the duct tape and gutter seal my dad put around the windows.

My future? David was it. I wanted to finish my degree, own a house, have a family. Marriage to him would make all that possible. When we got engaged, the diamond was as big as my fantasy. I had it all.

I lost it two months later. While I was out trying on wedding dresses, he was sleeping with other women. The only thing worse than finding out he was cheating on me was finding out at a bowling alley. He had been acting strangely for days, so I bluntly asked, half joking, "What, are you cheating on me?" When he didn't answer, I stormed away. Then I decided, No, I'm not going home to boo-hoo all alone. I went back to him, yelled at him, even grabbed him by the collar and ripped his designer shirt. I didn't like him, but worse, I didn't like the person I had become.

It was over. I gave him back the ring and told him to give it to me when he wanted me and me alone. I never got that ring back. I got something better.

I got angry. Angry at him. Angry at me. Angry enough to get my own act together.

I was 26. It was time to grow up. When I broke up with

him, I broke up with the person I no longer wanted to be. It was time to take charge of me and my life.

Without David, the future was blank. It was up to me to write something on it. It was time to own my life. First, I returned everything he left in my house—including the *Playboy* magazines he had hidden in my dresser. I exchanged the sexy miniskirt and slinky black dress he bought me for sensible skirts and slacks I could wear to a career job. Then I got a college catalog and opened it. I had no idea what I wanted to be or do, but I did know this: I wanted to be happy.

That's when the world opened up. Everything in my life changed when I decided to change me. I didn't need to *find* the right person. I needed to *become* the right person.

Burying your talents won't make them grow.

One day in high school we all took an aptitude test to see what we were destined to be. We laughed at the results. I was supposed to be a respiratory therapist. My friend Betsy was supposed to be a truck driver.

Betsy ended up working as a nurse. I ended up a writer.

Who knew?

Somewhere inside, we did.

Somewhere inside, we all know.

We just do a great job of burying our deepest passions.

I did everything in my power to avoid using my talents. I buried them as deep as I could and I resisted anyone who came at me, with a shovel. In ninth grade, my English teacher, Mr. Ricco, made us write a paragraph each week. I balked. I wrote mine right before class and picked the most boring subjects to wear him down. Instead, he wore me down and polished me into a writer without my knowing it.

Still, I resisted. I never wrote for the high school newspaper or yearbook or took any creative writing classes. I was too scared of the one thing I desperately wanted to be: a writer. So many of us know deep inside that one thing we were meant to do, would love to do; but it's too scary to actually do it because we might fail at it, so we leave it buried inside where it will be safe, untouched and untapped. The dream and desire to do it seem so much safer than actually taking action and risking failure and rejection.

I wrote in secret, filling diaries and journals. One day, out of bravery or ignorance, I let my sisters read them. Later, when I realized what I had done, I took the diaries to the metal trash drum in the backyard and burned them. As the flames ate my words, it seemed they were putting out the fire in me.

The embers still burned. In tenth grade, when I read Henry David Thoreau, something in my soul expanded. It was like I could take in more breath. I didn't have enough money to buy my own copy of *Walden*, so I copied the text from the school's copy word for word, starting with why he went into the woods.

To avoid writing, I almost ended up in the woods for a living. We've all heard that saying "Man plans, God laughs." Had my plans been blessed by the gods, I would have ended up a forest ranger. I was too scared to be a writer, so I turned to conservation for a college major when I turned away from writing. How ironic that I ended up as a journalist filling newspapers and books with words. I pray that those forest rangers preserve enough trees to keep me in business.

I have loved newspapers ever since I was a toddler sitting on the floor near my father's steel-toed work boots as he buried his face in the daily news. I pretended to read whatever section he dropped on the floor, curious about what mesmerized my dad after a long day spent patching up a hot roof. When my mom had time to read, which was close to never while raising 11 children, she loved newspaper columnist Erma Bombeck. Erma made writing look so easy. And it was, in my diary. There it stayed, safe and sound, for years.

I buried my talents out of fear they would never be good enough. I ignored the call to use my talents. I kept telling God I wasn't ready, until one day it hit me: What if God stopped asking? What's scarier than God calling you to use your talents is the thought that God will stop calling you and go elsewhere.

The parable of the talents in the Bible haunted me. A nobleman gave one of his servants five talents, another one two, and another man one talent. As time went on, the man with the five talents traded with them and made five more talents. The one with two talents doubled his as well. The man with one talent dug a hole in the ground and hid the money out of fear. When the master came back, he rewarded the first two men. The man who buried his talent returned it unused. The master was angry, took the talent, and tossed the servant out. The master told the first two men: "To everyone who has will more be given, and he will have an abundance; you have been faithful over a little, therefore I will make you lord over much" (see Matthew 25).

When you have been faithful with what you have been given, you get more. You won't get more talents until you use what you've already been given.

We're all gifted, but some people never open their packages. We each have a calling, a vocation, a particular unique talent. Your calling isn't necessarily your job title. It might not be written on the business card you carry, or on your job description, or on your résumé. It's more likely written on your heart. I worked a lot of jobs before I found that place in life that writer Frederick Buechner calls "the place where your deep gladness and the world's deep hunger meet."

What does God want you to do with the gifts He gave you? Use them. Not hoard them. When the Israelites got hungry on their way to the Promised Land, God dropped manna from heaven. Free bread! Out of fear, the people hoarded the bread for the next day. It grew moldy. God wanted them to have faith that each day's grace would be enough.

No hoarding. You have to use up all you have learned, uncovered, and discovered, or you don't get more. My writing had to have life beyond my bedroom. But who would want to read it? Who would publish it? Who would buy it? That was all none of my business. It was time to take action. In prayer I might have been saying yes to God, but a yes without action isn't truly a yes.

What are you called to do or be? The answer is in you. Instead of conducting a survey of family and friends about what you should do, survey the inner landscape to find the spiritual interpretation of your life. God has already whispered it to you. Most of us keep our lives too busy and noisy to listen.

Many of us stay clueless not because we don't know, but because we're afraid of knowing, because then we'll have to take action. I was at a party once and listened to a woman complaining to the small crowd around her that she had all these career options and just couldn't choose. Every time someone offered a great piece of advice, she rejected it instantly and said, "I don't know what to do." She was getting a lot of attention and mileage out of not knowing, out of being helpless.

I felt that tug of the Spirit, looked her in the eye, and gently asked, "Do you *want* to know?"

She looked appalled. Everyone grew quiet. Then she softened. "Yes," she said, and proceeded to tell all of us exactly what she loved but was afraid of doing.

Someone once told me this beautiful story: Before we arrive in this world, we each possess all the wisdom we will ever need for this life and beyond. But right before we're born, an angel comes and touches us on the lips, as if to silence us, and leaves an imprint there, causing us to forget everything we knew. We spend the rest of our lives recovering the lost data.

Sometimes I place my finger on my upper lip, right in that little groove, and listen.

Try it. It will remind you to stop talking so you can listen to the wisdom you already possess.

*What they call you is up to them. What you
answer to is up to you.*

People do it all the time. Ask someone, "What do you do
for a living?" and they'll use that nasty four-letter word *just*.

"I'm just a janitor."

"I'm just an orderly."

"I'm just a bus driver."

"I'm just a secretary."

Just?

I love when I run into people who can't wait to tell you
what they do for a living. They create their own job titles and
celebrate who they are. The woman who paints nails who calls
herself a Nail Technician. The guy who repairs pianos whose
business card identifies him as Director of Piano Technology.
The man at the amusement park who fixes the merry-go-
round and sees himself as a Ride Technician. The person who
cleans the city pool who calls herself the Aquatics Manager.

The hotel security worker who calls himself Director of Loss Prevention.

What's in a title?

Nothing and everything. It all depends on what the title is, who gave it to you, and whether it expands or limits you. Instead of shrinking to fit a job title, sometimes you have to expand the box you're in and create a title that fits.

The key is to do what's in the job title you have and squeeze in room to do what matches the job title you want to have.

When I was hired to be a business reporter at the *Beacon Journal* in Akron, I cried the whole drive home. I wanted the salary and benefits, but I didn't want to be a business reporter. I didn't want to write about sales figures, annual meetings, and quarterly earnings reports. I hated numbers and data. They didn't fit the mantra pounded into us in journalism school: "Bring me humans!" Where were the humans in the stock listings and statistics?

It was my job to find them, so I did. I wrote business news but also created a side beat spotlighting people who worked interesting jobs. I wrote about a chimney sweep, a cement truck driver, and a blimp pilot. I did magazine stories on third-shift workers and farmers, and followed a woman all the way through the police academy.

Not everyone appreciated my zeal at first, but they usually liked the final product. Too many bosses put people in a box. Whatever box they put you in, expand it. Better yet, break down the sides, smash it to the floor, and turn that box into a wide-open blank slate and write whatever you want on it.

Don't ask. Just do it. As they say, it's better to ask forgiveness than to ask permission. Every morning before work, decide who you want to be and go be it. It's up to you, no one else. No one except you is in charge of building your résumé, or giving you challenging work, or making your nine-to-five day meaningful.

Before I got the dream job of being a newspaper columnist, I used to tell people, "I'm a columnist without a column." It helped me see past the position I had as a reporter to the position I wanted. I love those famous words by poet Lucille Clifton: "What they call you is one thing; what you answer to is something else." That part is up to you.

When I was growing up, my next-door neighbor, Thelma, worked in the kitchen at the hospital. She was my mom's age, and I felt sorry for her because she spent her whole career in a hospital kitchen wearing a pink uniform and a hairnet, until I realized why. Her job title might have been Kitchen Help, but Thelma considered herself so much more than that. She made the best piecrust in town. What a treat for patients. It didn't matter what her title was. She considered herself a baker.

I thought of Thelma when I was asked to speak at a ceremony honoring Cleveland Clinic employees with 25 years of service. It could have been a boring night; it could have been little more than an assembly line of handshakes, photos, and watches handed out. It could have been a ho-hum night of identical thank-yous to 200 workers. They could have been treated like cogs in the massive medical machine that is the Cleveland Clinic.

Instead, it was like opening a treasure chest filled with something more valuable than jewels. Each person was seen for what they were: a vital player in saving lives and enhancing the quality of patients', families', and coworkers' lives.

They had all started at the hospital before computers, when bills were hand-typed, when nurses wore white caps, when no one paid for parking. Back then, offices were the size of elevators; some actually were in old elevators.

On this night when they were honored, you couldn't tell the doctors from the medical-records workers in the ballroom. It didn't matter what anyone's paycheck or title was. On this night, everyone was equal. Everyone had given their 25 best years. The program carried a bio on each employee, but it wasn't the stuff of résumés. It was the stuff that truly matters: *Consistently jovial. Pleasant conversations. Boundless energy. Wonderful storyteller. Humble.*

The program mentioned that one department coordinator for the Cancer Center was often found at her desk late into the night trying to schedule patients. One person whom we'd call a custodian didn't just clean offices; he helped visitors find their way. The fire marshal was more than that. He was a human alarm clock who drove every day from Columbus to Cleveland his first year of work and was always on time. That's a two-and-a-half-hour drive—one way.

A pediatrician was praised for his "Daffy Duck" voice that quieted the most frightened child into laughing through medical exams. He was also praised for his work getting bicycle helmet safety legislation passed. One nurse was referred to as an actor, comedian, and published author. She was also known as the Nurse Whisperer. What did she whisper? Probably, "Get well, get well, get well."

They talked about a dentist whose specialty was facial prosthetic replacements. He gave patients a new way to face life with new eyes, ears, noses, and mouths. Because of him, patients could enjoy a drink, a meal, a kiss.

The man who maintained dry-goods storage and ordered supplies made sure the babies didn't go hungry. He was vigilant about making sure there were always enough tube feedings and infant formula on hand.

I left the celebration knowing that the custodians of the world matter as much as the heart surgeons, that it doesn't matter what the world calls us. We get to decide who we really are. And it's up to each of us to take the word *just* out of our job titles.

In this drama of life, there are no small parts.

Thinking small stops too many of us from doing great things. We talk ourselves out of doing a kindness because we figure someone else will do it or because we doubt we can pull it off.

Folks on the bottom rung sometimes feel that way: the invisible workers in cubicles, the title-less people in accounts receivable, the nameless voices on the phones in billing. But a handful of those people changed a man's life one week. Changed it forever.

It all started when Marty Kenny lost his right hand in a car accident one summer night back in 2003. One friend left him to die on a bridge in the industrial Flats of Cleveland while another friend stayed and saved his life.

That summer day in June started out as a celebration of friendship. Marty and Dean Stecker spent the day hanging vinyl siding, pounding nails in the hot sun. They ended up at a party and left with Marty's friend Greg.

Greg drove them all to a bar in the Flats. When they left the bar at 11:30 p.m., Greg revved the engine and spun in the gravel. The car was going 60 in a 25-mile-an-hour zone when he floored it. Marty yelled for him to slow down, then gripped the door with his hand and held on for dear life. The car hit a dip in the road and went airborne on a lift bridge.

BAM!

The car slammed into the wall of the bridge so hard, it flipped over and skidded on the passenger side across the steel bridge. It screamed across the serrated metal like a train. When the car stopped 240 feet away on its side, Dean crawled out a window. Marty was stuck under the car. His right hand was gone.

Dean pushed hard to flip the car over, back onto its wheels, to free Marty. Greg walked around dazed, his business cards falling through the grate into the water like confetti. Dean tore off his shirt and wrapped it around Marty's arm. He screamed for Greg to call 911. He watched in shock as Greg paused to pick up the side mirror to his car, then drove away with the only cell phone. Hope faded as the red taillights disappeared into the night.

Dean wrapped both arms and legs around his bleeding buddy as they sat on a bridge suspended over the Cuyahoga River. Marty lost so much blood, it drained through the steel bridge like rainwater. Dean cradled Marty, rocking him as if that could stop the bleeding. Both of them were soaked in his blood.

On that dark, lonely bridge in Cleveland's industrial Flats,

Dean screamed at Marty to hold on, to stay conscious. When Marty fell silent, Dean rocked him and told him everything a dying man should hear: "Your wife loves you, your son loves you, and I love you."

Then he heard a rumble and saw headlights. Dean set Marty down and jumped in front of the vehicle and started screaming for help. The driver called paramedics. Dean's tourniquet saved Marty's life, but there was no hope for his hand.

Later on in the courtroom, the judge held up photos of Marty's injured arm as Greg stood with his two good hands cuffed behind his back. Marty stared at those hands with envy, with anger, with sadness. Greg was convicted of aggravated vehicular assault. In the courtroom, Marty reached over to hold his wife's hand, only he didn't have one, so she laced her fingers over the stub of his arm and held it.

For four months, the 21-year-old struggled to tie his shoes, write a check, diaper his newborn daughter, have a catch with his 4-year-old son. He lived off the money he and his wife had saved to fix up their house.

I stood on the bridge where he lost his hand when he visited the scene for the first time. He ran his fingers across the ser-rated grating of the bridge, studied the skid marks, and peered through at the river.

"I'm looking for my hand," he joked, only I could tell he wasn't completely joking. He had left a part of himself there. Marty can't remember much about that night. Dean can't forget.

I wrote a long article about the accident, about their friend-ship, about Dean's efforts to save him. The two celebrated the court case being over. They sat at Marty's dining room table and shoved aside stacks of medical bills that Medicaid would cover as long as Marty didn't work and his wife didn't earn too much at her day-care job. But he wasn't sure how to cover the prosthetic hand he wanted. His son wanted his dad to get a robotic arm so he could give him a high five. Dean worried that Marty would get discouraged that he couldn't swing a bat, tie a fishing lure, or hold both of his children's hands at once.

When the story about Marty went public, the paper-pushers and phone operators in the gray cubicles at Hanger Prosthetics & Orthotics in South Euclid, Ohio, couldn't forget his face. And that missing hand. When Lisa Kowardy first saw Marty's picture in the paper, she felt awful. "It was a terrible inhumanity done to him," she said. "We wanted to show him some humanity."

Who is Lisa?

She shrugs. "I'm just the billing manager."

Just?

Her job was to juggle accounts receivable. She never saw the patients, only their bills.

After she read about Marty, she and the women around her, women crammed into a small office above a storage room, approached management to do something about it. Lisa copied the news article and gave it to Kimberly Reed, the woman in charge of fitting prosthetics. Another woman tracked down Marty.

All of the women upstairs—Charon Speights, Alida Van Horn, Irene Flanik, Rose Johnson, and Annette Phillips— wanted to help Marty swing a bat with his son and be able to feed his baby daughter a bottle.

Because of their diligence and dedication, Marty got a $58,000 robotic hand for free.

The TV cameras captured Marty trying out his new hand, picking up a tissue, signing his name, lifting a bottle. The cameras didn't stay to capture Marty thanking the women who made it happen. The women oohed and ahhed when Marty came up to show off his hand.

"All you lovely people, this is just amazing," Marty said. "You guys are great."

Marty couldn't stop opening and closing his hand and talking about how powerful it was, with 22 pounds of pinch pressure.

"Do that guy thing and scratch yourself," Lisa joked.

"Not with this hand." Marty laughed.

He rolled up his sleeve to show it off.

"Oh my God, it's beautiful," Irene said.

"This is more than I could ever imagine," Marty said as they all fought back tears.

He promised to come back with his wife and two kids, then raised his new hand and waved good-bye, as if it were nothing at all.

Give others a second chance to make a first impression.

They always say, "You never have a second chance to make a first impression."

Thank goodness people have been gracious enough to give me a slew of second chances.

I've made a lot of bad first impressions. The first time I stepped into a newsroom as a student guest to meet with my mentor, I wore a black blouse with silver glittery stripes, a ruffled collar, and sleeves that poofed out at the shoulders like balloons. A white gauzy skirt, a pair of black hose, and bright white shoes completed the ensemble. Someone should have called the fashion police to throw the book at me.

I came back two years later for a job interview there. This time, I meant business. I wore the only suit I owned. So much was riding on that interview at the *Beacon Journal* in Akron. I was 30, a single mom with no money and big dreams. I wanted to be a real journalist, the kind that could pay the rent from a writing job. I had blown my first impressions when I tried to get an internship. At the *Pittsburgh Press*, an editor asked about my hobbies and interests. I told him about my love for violin music but choked when he asked me about Isaac Stern an hour later. My mind went blank. I had also blown a shot at an internship at the *Detroit Free Press*. An editor liked my résumé and asked me to write an essay. I wrote a powerful essay on a lousy typewriter. I had to pencil in corrections. The editor never called back. Finally, after 30 rejection letters, a small paper in Lorain, Ohio, the *Lorain Journal*, gave me an internship in 1986 that turned into a job.

Sometimes we're the ones who need a second chance; sometimes it's up to us to grant one. Sometimes it's both. That was the case with the toughest boss I ever had.

The stories about him were legendary. Most of them were true. Trash cans flew. Heads rolled. Grown men cried. My first editor, John Cole, was Lou Grant on steroids. He gave me the desk that sat under a warning bell that went off when we were on deadline. That bell wasn't as bad as sitting right outside his door at the *Lorain Journal*. Everyone feared the wrath of John. He fired people and hired them back, sometimes in the same day.

One day he hated what he saw in the newspaper so he stood on a desk in the middle of the newsroom, let loose a long rant about how he might as well just give up and die, then lay down on the floor.

One time a photographer showed him a feature photo of a nun in full habit splashing around Lake Erie.

"What do you think of this?" John asked me. Trick question. Did *he* like it?

"Um, it's interesting?" I answered.

"No it isn't," John said. "It's a cliché." Then he tore the photo to shreds and let the tiny pieces fall on the photographer's feet.

John was tough. He made us tougher. He was the kind of boss who changes you forever. Years later, you still bear the imprint—and the scars. He became editor of the paper when he was 29. The people who worked with him used the same words to describe him: *mercurial, demanding, smart, fearless, passionate, no-nonsense, gruff.* They called him a crusader with contempt for corruption, who celebrated the truth and never cowered before anyone.

John stood up for us. I often heard him on the phone yelling to a source, "Those are my reporters. If you have a problem with my reporter, you have a problem with me."

End of problem.

When I was still brand-new, one day another reporter dumped a story in my lap that he had been assigned but didn't want. It would involve working another late night on top of my assignment to cover city hall. I wiped away tears at my desk.

"Brett, get in here," John yelled.

He challenged me to get tougher. "There's no crying in my newsroom," he barked. Oh, if he only knew how much crying went on in his newsroom.

"Don't let people push you around," he yelled.

Strange, but I left his office feeling better, like he had given me an espresso shot of courage. Then he called that reporter in. I tried not to smile as I heard the screaming. A few minutes later, the reporter came to my desk and, without looking at me, asked to take back his assignment and told me, "John said you can go home."

John cared about the right things. He taught me that you're never too small to make a difference and never too big to be gracious about it.

I'd worked for him only six months when the phone rang one day on deadline. John sat the new person under the warning bell. The bell was ready to go off when a secretary handed me a phone message with a name I didn't recognize. I called back and John Greenman from the *Beacon Journal* answered. He wasn't part of the story I was writing, so I told him I was on deadline and hung up.

Then it hit me: *Oh no, I just killed my future*. I had just hung up on an editor who worked for a newspaper I wanted to work for. Another terrible first impression.

When I called back, he told me he was impressed that I put the deadline first and wanted me to come in for an interview.

That year, 1986, Akron's largest employer, Goodyear, was in the midst of a takeover attempt by Sir James Goldsmith. The paper directed all its best business writers to cover that big story. The paper needed another business writer to cover the less important news.

I knew nothing about the business world. I'd never read a business section before, so I was completely unprepared. I showed up in my one and only business suit to look as smart and professional as possible. No black-and-white disaster outfit this time. They ushered me into the editor's office. It was full of men wearing yellow power ties. The interview went well until the editor of the newspaper asked me how I would write a profile of Martin Marietta.

I'd never heard of the guy, but gave a detailed account of how I would gather background on Mr. Marietta. Then I noticed the editor looked like he was ready to deliver a kidney stone. They were all cringing as I went on and on about Mr. Marietta. Finally, one of them broke the news: Martin Marietta wasn't a person. It was a major defense corporation.

Arghhh! I felt so stupid. I had prayed going into the interview and all through it had held my right hand open and pretended to be holding on to God's hand. Now what? I prayed, took a deep breath, and said something like, "Well, it's obvious I don't know the business world, so if you need an experienced business writer, I'm not the one to hire. But I do know how to report and write, and I'm willing to learn anything I need to know for the job."

They were kind and shook my hand. One of them escorted me to the elevator. As I pushed the button, my heart sank. I'd probably just blown the best chance I would ever get to work for a great newspaper. Before the elevator door opened, the managing editor came over and asked when I could start work.

What? They were going to hire me anyway?

And they did.

I found out later they hired a copy editor who spelled her name wrong on her résumé. So much for first impressions.

It was hard to break the news to my editor in Lorain that I was leaving after just six months on the job, my first real career job.

When I left his newspaper, John Cole wished me well but didn't say much. A week later, my mom called. John Cole had sent my parents a letter, telling them what a great job *they* had done.

Every job is as magical as you make it.

W hat's the worst job you ever had? That's always a great conversation starter. Go ahead, ask people. But you have to be careful. Your worst job could be someone else's best job.

Wouldn't it be great to have a cosmic job swap? If everyone gave up the job they hated, someone who truly loved that job could step in and be happy.

My worst job? Picking up bodies for a funeral home.

When you work at a funeral home, you do a little bit of everything. You print memorial cards, wash hearses, work viewing hours, and go out on death calls. You never forget your first dead body. The first time I was "on call" I had no idea what to expect. You just go to sleep at night and the phone rings if they need you. The call came at 3 a.m. It was eerie driving a hearse in the dead of night (pun intended) to claim a body.

The woman was in her 40s and had thick black hair.

Decades have passed and I still remember her face. She was in bed and her eyes were still open. She had been ill for some time, and the family doctor had already been to the house to pronounce her dead. The family was present, so I had to act like it didn't bother me in the least to touch her. I didn't realize how hard it was to lift a dead body until I tried to lift her. It gave new meaning to the word *deadweight*. Back at the funeral home, we had to undress her, rinse off her body, and position her head and hands for viewing hours.

At times, the funeral business can be deeply disturbing. Week after week, you're immersed in death and grief. You have to handle decomposing bodies that hadn't been found for weeks that no longer look human. You have to cover the holes left in bodies by guns but are helpless to fill the holes left in the survivors of those suicides. The smell of death makes you gag until it's replaced by the smell of embalming fluid, which makes your eyes water. But nothing bothers you more than the tiny coffins. The newborns, the stillborns, the hopes and dreams for a lifetime that ended with an empty nursery and numb parents who aren't sure they can still call themselves parents.

The magical part?

Seeing death up close gives you a deep appreciation for life. One day an embalmer allowed me to assist him. He showed me how years of unhealthy eating can narrow the artery in your neck. I've never forgotten seeing the cross section of that man's thick artery. I think of it every time I'm tempted to eat a French fry.

One day I walked into the embalming room to be greeted by a man whose chest was spread apart like an open book.

His body had been autopsied and the embalmer had opened it to prepare it. For a brief second I was horrified and jumped back. Then I was completely fascinated. I stepped closer and examined each rib and the tissue that had once held his beating heart in place. It was a beautiful moment. How often do you get to peer inside a human body?

Over the years, I've interviewed hundreds of people, from blimp pilots to migrant workers and everyone in between. They all had jobs one person might love and another person might hate. I spent weeks talking to migrant workers at a muck farm in Hartville, Ohio. They had a job I assumed most people would hate.

The women I talked to said they preferred to be called field-workers. They didn't call themselves migrants. They didn't like the stigma that job title gave them. One woman told me the word *migrant* conjured up images of poor, dirty, uneducated people to be pitied. "They call us migrants, but I don't see us as that. I like to cut lettuce. It's an honest pay," she said. "If I don't want to work, I don't have to. I just get paid less."

The workers came from as far as South Carolina, Florida, and Texas to work the muck fields at the K.W. Zellers & Son produce farm in Hartville, Ohio. They brought their children, their work clothes, and their Bibles. They moved into old farmhouses, shanties, and trailers. They wore bright yellow waterproof overalls that matched their yellow rain slickers and rode old school buses deep into the fields on the 400-acre farm. They planted and cut Bibb lettuce, romaine, and endive that glowed fluorescent against the black earth. They tucked their hair into bright bandannas and wide straw hats, squeezed fingers into orange latex gloves, and rubber-banded their ankles to keep bugs from crawling up their pant legs, then shoved their feet into black rubber boots.

Every day they were one with nature. Their music was the crunch of knees crawling in unison, the swish of cold knives against warm green lettuce, and soft songs to Jesus rising from the sombreros. I heard row upon row of hearty laughter.

I spent one day picking onions with them and came home with a killer backache. When I blew my nose, dirt came out. I couldn't last a day doing that work. They never complained. They rejoiced over a bird's nest they found in the field. They checked on that nest every day and shared updates on the mother bird and the babies.

They used rubber bands to create bouquets of red radishes. They never stopped for rain, no matter how hard it fell, or the sun, no matter how hot it felt. When the baking sun was too much, the women giggled and ran through the irrigation sprinklers. They tossed handfuls of lettuce at one another. They chattered about love affairs on soap operas. They talked about where they would spend their money at the mall. They told me they preferred the sun, wind, and sky to any indoor job. They pitied people stuck in an office all day with a glass window between them and the world.

"It makes you feel like you are free, like you're not locked up all the time," Willa Mae told me.

They taught me that every job is as magical as you make it. Sometimes the magic isn't in the paycheck or perks. It's in the mark you make or leave behind, from the nest in the field to the bouquets of red radishes that end up in the grocery store.

There's a time for everything but not always at the same time.

Early in my career as a journalist, a boss gave me a rude awakening about my dual roles. I was a single mom and an aspiring journalist, and I wanted to excel at both.

An editor came up to me in the newsroom one day excited to offer me an incredible opportunity to go out of state to cover a big breaking news story. He assumed I'd jump at the chance. What journalist wouldn't?

Me.

My daughter had one parent. Her dad wasn't involved in her life. I alone had to figure out child care. To find someone to spend a few nights watching her at a moment's notice seemed insurmountable. I told the editor that I couldn't give him an answer right that second. He gave me a sour look, shook his head, and said, "Brett, you're going to have to choose between being a mother and being a reporter."

Did I? How could I? I needed that job to support my daughter.

It was easy for him to compartmentalize his life and stay 100 percent focused at work. He had a wife at home running the house and caring for their child.

Way back then, I wanted to be a powerhouse in the newsroom, but I also wanted to be the best mother in the world. How could I do both? It seemed like the two didn't match. Juggling parenting and work is hard. Just when you have it down, it seems like someone tosses you a bowling ball and a raw egg to juggle in the mix.

I had already been passed over for one job because I was a single mom. Years before I was a journalist, a paving company needed a secretary who doubled as a dispatcher. I was made for the job. I had used a radio as an emergency medical technician and had been an office manager. Perfect. The company called my current employer and asked only one question: Does she miss work to take care of her child?

I didn't get the job.

How do you become a great parent and a great employee? Do you have to choose?

It wasn't until years later that I got clarity from a woman who told me, "You can have it all; you just can't have it all at the same time." Or maybe you can, just not in the same hour or day or week.

I once spoke at a retreat called BREATHE at Camp Robin Hood in, of all places, Freedom, New Hampshire. The women's weekend offered all sorts of healthy activities including hiking, biking, swimming, and canoeing. I ended up with a rifle in my hands at the shooting range. *Bam! Bam! Bam!*

It wasn't so much the power of the gun that thrilled me, but the focus and concentration that it took to hit that target 20 feet away. I gathered a handful of targets and used them for my presentation about how to stay focused on the bull's-eye and not get lost aiming for the outer rings of the target.

Jamie Cole, who organized the retreat, said she struggled with the idea of having just one target when it seemed she had so many targets that popped up at different times in her life, sometimes in the same day or hour. Her job, her children, her various passions. I thought about that dilemma we all share. What do you make your priority when everything and everyone seem to be the top priority?

I went back to the shooting range and found the answer. There was a target sheet that had not just one target printed on it, but five small ones. Each target had its own ring and its own bull's-eye. Sometimes you have to switch targets. Jamie loved it.

Instead of feeling as though she had one target in life and had to put her children or her work in the outer rings, she could put them all in the bull's-eye, just not on the same target.

We talked about how, when you're at work, you aim for the work bull's-eye. You stay focused on the task, the project, the job, the bottom line. We often do have different targets at the same time, and sometimes they're all moving at once.

I've learned to stop and assess which target just showed up in my life. I pause and reenter my life with different intentions hour by hour. When I used to host a weekly radio show, I paused, rebooted, and reminded myself I was about to interview someone so I needed to listen carefully and be present.

When I visit my grandbabies, I pause, reboot, and remind myself I am their wickedly fun grandma who is here to play, read, wrestle, and build forts.

Each time I enter a new segment of my life, I pause, reboot, and claim that identity. I make sure I'm in the right segment, being the right me, hour by hour, chunk by chunk. It's a way of consecrating my life, to make myself present and to make each encounter a holy one.

Each time I reaffirm: What is the bull's-eye on this particular target? Best parent. Best boss. Best grandma. I no longer bring work to do when I visit my grandbabies. I no longer check e-mail while playing LEGOs. When you're at home, you aim for the parenting bull's-eye. When you're with your children, you're with them, 100 percent. Turn off the Black-Berry, iPhone, iPad, and e-mail, and be fully present.

When my brain gets jumbled over priorities or jolted back and forth between them, I pause and decide which target is top priority at that very moment, then focus on that one with all the energy and passion I have in me to hit the bull's-eye.

None of us will ever do it all, or do it all perfectly. I'll never forget the tsunami of scorn that hit over presidential candidate Mitt Romney's wife, Ann, who raised five sons. Some women scoffed and said Ann "never worked a day in her life." The Mommy Wars heated up, even though we all know that anyone with five sons worked *every* day of her life.

It hit that nuclear button: Am I enough? There's a war waged within every mom. Am I doing enough for my children if I work outside the home? Am I doing enough for myself and for the world if I don't?

If that wasn't bad enough, one week *Time* magazine had

the audacity to ask on its cover: *Are you mom enough?* It didn't help that the cover photo was of a sexy, young mom in skinny jeans nursing a three-year-old son pressed against her bare breast. The picture of the woman disturbed some people, but the question the headline posed should disturb us all.

Are you mom enough?

Many days the answer we would give ourselves would be no.

Like the day my little girl held up her spoonful of Cheerios to show me the little worm wiggling on it. *Oh no, when did that box of cereal expire?* Or the afternoon I took a moment to sit in a lawn chair to crack open a book and my toddler bolted into the street. Or the time I went to get her out of the crib and found her playing with what had rolled out of the diaper I failed to seal shut. Or the morning I found her eating a stick of butter for breakfast after she learned how to open the refrigerator door. Or the time I had to pry her fingers off the car door in the grade school parking lot when she developed a fear of going to school. She didn't know I cried harder than she did after I pulled away to go to work.

If we're keeping score on parenting, it might seem that we're all failures some days. My daughter is parenting more perfectly than I ever did. She taught her babies to self-soothe, swaddled them like burritos, hand-painted onesies, and sewed ribbons onto burp cloths. She even decided to leave her career to be a full-time mom.

There are days she calls in tears, sometimes from the joy, sometimes from the guilt over mothering a three-year-old and a ten-month-old. Is she a good-enough mom when a tired

Asher cries for his "striped blankie" and begs her to turn the car around to get it and she doesn't? Or when she lets Ainsley cry herself to sleep because sleep is what that tired baby needs most?

There's no perfect parent. Not the ones who stay home all day. Not the ones who go to work. Not the ones who carefully sterilize every bottle and nipple. Not the ones who breast-feed until the child is taking the SAT.

I remember one day my mom gave herself an F for parenting. She was fretting all day because my little brother forgot his lunch and she blamed herself. I remember thinking, *Wow, she cares that much about us?* My mom did the best she could raising 11 children. Some days she hit it out of the ballpark. Some days she hit a single. Some days she struck out. But she always got up to bat, no matter how exhausted she felt.

Baseball offers a good way to measure success. A great batting average is .300. That means 70 percent of the time, you fail. Even the greatest home-run hitters strike out. Some of the greatest players of all time are included in the list of the 100 major-league players with the most strikeouts: Reggie Jackson, Hank Aaron, Willie Mays, Babe Ruth, Mickey Mantle, Sammy Sosa, and Barry Bonds. The year Babe Ruth set the record for most home runs in a season, he also struck out more times than any other player in the majors. How comforting.

Every mom is playing in the major leagues. We have the most important job in the world. The reason we strike out is because every day we step up to home plate and swing with all we've got.

Are we mom enough?

You bet.

Every single one of us is doing the best we can.

So let's call a truce in the Mommy Wars both around us and inside us. No more judgments about what we "should" be doing. Let's stop "shoulding" all over ourselves and one another.

Let's just do the best we can and call it enough.

Only you can determine your worth.

"Would you like fries with that?"

You get used to asking that with every order.

I worked at McDonald's for only one week, but it left an imprint for life.

Since one out of every eight Americans have worked at a McDonald's, a newspaper editor asked me to get hired at McDonald's and write a story about it for Labor Day.

I was honest with the manager at the nearest McDonald's and told her I was a newspaper reporter. I asked her to treat me the same as everyone else. No special privileges. That meant I had to go through the interview, sit through orientation, and wear the McUniform, which was two sizes too large.

It's hard to get nervous about applying for a job when the flip side of the application is a Ronald McDonald summer fun safety maze to color. The place mats doubled as job applications. I got hired to work the hours of 7 a.m. to 2 p.m. At orientation, I got a McDonald's bag with two uniforms. We watched training films on how to wash our hands and on how to treat customers. TLC meant "think like a customer." We were never to use the term "fast food." We were a "quick service" restaurant.

Once home I opened the bag and pulled out the black polyester pants; a red, gray, and blue striped polo shirt; and a bright red hat with a huge *M* and the words "We Got the Power." The hat stuck up five inches off my head. My daughter laughed hysterically and dared me to put the uniform on in front of her. At least it was one outfit she wouldn't ask to borrow.

Each day I had to clock in five minutes before my shift. The small employee lounge had signs all over to remind us: Talk To Our Customers, Smile, and Learn Customers' First Names.

The manager popped in a video for me to watch called *Serving Up Smiles* on how to make breakfast. Everything I fixed was supposed to look like the pictures and be served in 59 seconds or less.

I ended up working at the drive-thru window. Robbin trained me. She wanted to change the world and used her 30 seconds with each customer to do so. She could tell who was in a hurry, who needed a compliment, who needed to feel important. She knew the names of the regulars and punched in their orders before they gave them. She looked past the yawning, grumpy, unshaven faces and smiled.

"I usually look into their eyes and watch them for the expression on their faces to tell how they're feeling and what they're thinking," she told me.

When people found out she was 31 and worked at McDonald's they pitied her. She didn't see why. She was proud of her work. She was saving up to buy a house.

It was hard work. My knees and feet ached from standing all day. There was nowhere to sit. To amuse myself, I looked into people's cars, checking out what was hanging from the rearview mirror (fuzzy dice, air fresheners, clocks) and what oddities were in the backseat (a vacuum, a roll of carpet, golf clubs). We could never sit except for our 30-minute break. My feet felt like they would explode. My hands smelled like grease. My uniform stuck to me. Before going home I filled fry baskets with frozen potatoes. I left exhausted.

The next day I worked the front counter. We were supposed to greet everyone with: "Welcome to McDonald's. May I take your order?" But we got so busy, I started shouting, "Next!" The person training me that day was Carlos, who was 17. He was 20 years younger than me but never made me feel small. He knew too well what that can be like. He rolled his eyes when one manager told him to send me to the dining room to clean tables. "I won't send you, I'll ask you," he said. He refused to be a hen in the pecking order where I was the smallest chick. To him, we were all equals on a team.

Carlos wanted to be a doctor one day and work with crack babies in the neonatal unit. He was saving money for medical school. He worked 35 hours a week and graduated from high school a year early. McDonald's taught him responsibility, he said.

Between orders we stuffed dwarfs into Snow White Happy

Meal boxes and endlessly wiped off the counter. The motto was, "You lean, you clean." You can't afford to not look busy. I did that once and ended up cleaning the women's restroom. How solid waste can end up on the wall—the wall!—is beyond me. It was my job to scrub it off. I left that day smelling like bleach.

That night I attended a mandatory crew rally. It was like a pep assembly, complete with balloons, crepe paper, and food—from McDonald's of course. It was a chance to point out problems (like customers not getting condiments in the drive-thru); win prizes for McTrivia questions (What is the weight of a McDonald's sundae? Five ounces); and get answers to rare questions (What if a customer wants 18 packets of croutons for one salad?). They reminded us to use Mr. Tongs and Mr. Gloves, not fingers, to pick up food. They discussed the courtesy cards; 95 percent of the customers said the restrooms were unclean. (The cards must have been filled out before I cleaned.)

The next day at Mickey D's was meat day. They put me, a vegetarian, on the grill. I stared at sizzling sausage and bacon all morning. Then I moved to toasting muffins but kept forgetting to take them out when the machine buzzed. There were so many timers and buzzers and bells going off, I couldn't figure out which one went to which machine. It sounded like a science-fiction movie with a meltdown every ten seconds.

Sarah, the Grill Queen, showed me how to speed things up. She picked up four sausages at a time, using her fingers to keep them from falling. She had scars from her fingertips to her elbows from splattering grease. She opened the place at 4 a.m. and left at 1 p.m. She was 37 and had started at McDonald's as a teenager. Her dream was to own a restaurant. She loved working the grill.

"It's hard. It's nonstop. It'll make you or break you," she said.

At lunch, I assembled burgers, Big Macs, Quarter Pounders, and Triple Cheeseburgers. I thought a Triple Cheeseburger meant three pieces of cheese on one burger. Who in the world eats three beef patties?

Between 11:30 a.m. and 1 p.m. we were slammed. People called back special orders for dozens of burgers at once. We were supposed to use tongs to pick up the meat, but they slow you down. I tried wearing plastic gloves, but my fingers stuck together. So I used my bare hands and burned my fingertips.

The next day, they put me at the front drive-thru window where people picked up orders. All I had to do was hand food out a window. What could be easier? No one told me about the language barrier. The computer screen above me read: SACHBI, SAMFEG, SAEGBI. It took an hour to decipher the code: SA = sausage; BI = biscuit; MF = muffin; EG = egg; CH = cheese. What was a VANCON? Vanilla cone. For breakfast? Yep. I wasn't the only nutritionally challenged person who liked ice cream before noon.

Kay, my trainer for the day, reminded me to fold the bag tops, not crumple them, and not to lean on the window. She didn't even yell when I dropped an order between the car and the window. Kay was 37, had two kids, and had worked at McDonald's for 12 years.

"I love it," she said. "It's tough, but living on welfare doesn't make it."

Turnover is high. Most employees quit to go to college or

find other work. Some can't handle the stress. On my last day, I could see why.

One customer plopped his toddler son on the counter and ordered a triple cheeseburger. Then he told me I got it wrong. He wanted a value meal. So I got that. Then he said I got that wrong. He wanted the value meal without cheese on the burgers. Then he complained about that. The manager had to unjam my machine five times. I nearly violated number 7 of the McDonald's Ten Commandments: "Our customers are not people to argue or match wits with." This guy was lucky I didn't violate one of the original Ten Commandments: "Thou shalt not kill."

That customer saw me as some loser because I was working a fast-food job. It's a mistake many people make. They're wrong. It's noble work to feed people and lift the spirits of strangers. Martin Luther King Jr. was right when he said that all labor that uplifts humanity has dignity and importance.

Everyone I worked with at that McDonald's gave humanity a boost. They also knew to hold on to their own dignity. This wasn't menial work. It was a foundation for their dreams. Just ask former burger flippers Jay Leno, Star Jones, Shania Twain, Rachel McAdams, and Jeff Bezos, the founder of Amazon.

When my fast-food career at McDonald's ended, the owner asked me what I thought of working there. I told him to get rid of the hats, put a stool at the drive-thru window so employees could rest, and give everyone a big raise.

10

Even the mistakes belong.

Every creation starts with a lump of useless clay.

The potter leaves a part of himself in every creation.

Only the potter can hear the clay. He listens to know its breaking point, to learn its limitations, to reach past them or to accept them and make them a thing of beauty.

I've never tried my hand at clay but got to watch as Tom Gedeon sat at the potter's wheel, took a block of burnt-orange clay, squeezed it down then up, trying to keep it smooth and centered on the wheel. That's the key, he told me: stay centered.

The people who visit the Jesuit Retreat House in Cleveland seek the gift of the potter: staying centered and letting go as the Potter shapes your life.

At 78, Father Gedeon, whom everyone called Tom, still saw himself as the Potter's lump of clay. He could probably quote

Jeremiah 18:6: "Behold, as the clay is in the potter's hand, so are you in my hand." But he let the clay speak for him, not the Bible.

Ordained as a Jesuit priest in 1956, Tom ran the retreat house for 16 years, then traveled the country as executive director of Retreats International for 20 years. He started the professional organization that now connects more than 500 retreat houses in the United States and Canada.

After he retired, he joked that you can't say you're retired in religious life, so he called himself "an artist in residence." He puttered around this 57-acre sanctuary and tried, through his art, to help others hear the "universal call to holiness."

When he was the director there in 1962, he hung traditional religious art in the halls, Rembrandt-like depictions of Mary, Jesus, and churches.

"That's stuff I forced on people," he said, cringing.

When he returned in 2000, he took down all those "holy" pictures and hung his photographs. A lily pad in bloom, rowboats moored in a foggy cove, a flower poking through a drab gray fence: proof that even in the bleakness of life, beauty persists.

"These are the real holy pictures," he insisted. "Nature is God's greatest message of beauty."

Each captured a moment that delighted him, that he froze with his camera to delight others. He had taken pictures all his life, but he'd never touched clay until a nun suggested it a few years before. What a thrill to turn a mess of clay into a vase, a bowl, a teapot. He called art "the most primitive experience of God."

Off the garage, in a room the size of a toolshed, he had

just enough space to sit at the potter's wheel. His white wispy hair refused to behave in the humidity and poked out like Einstein's as he finished a bowl. The dish ended up with a slight dent only he could see.

"It's got some limitations," he said, but he wasn't disappointed. He was intrigued. It's been said that the Amish leave an imperfection in every quilt they create to remind them that only God creates with perfection. Tom didn't try to be perfect. He took joy in the imperfect.

Tom could tell by the coolness of the clay that it was time to flip the bowl over. He hesitated. It was the biggest one he had ever made, and he wasn't sure he could trust his aging hands with eight pounds of clay.

"If you want to see a grown man cry...," he warned as he flipped the bowl over. It didn't crack.

Even if it did, there's no such thing as a mistake to a potter. Or the Potter.

Once, when Tom used a stick to form a long neck in a vase, the clay bent, grabbed the stick, and wouldn't let go. A failure? Not at all. Everyone wanted to buy the disfigured vase.

The spinning clay pulls sweat from your hands, so the potter leaves a part of himself in every creation. Maybe that's why Tom always hated to let them go. He used to take a picture of each one, to hold it in his memory. He could have fetched more than the $20 or $30 he asked for each creation, but he wanted art to remain affordable to all. As the wheel turned slowly and another bowl spun, he talked about how grateful he was to delight others in his "closing years."

"Another ten years would be a great gift," he said.

He got only two more. He died in 2005, at 80. When I look

on the shelf in my living room at the vase he gave me, I think of how beautiful our flaws can be when we surrender like clay in the hands of the Potter.

It's hard to surrender. I keep striving for perfection as if it's attainable in all things when, in reality, most of the blessings that come to me, and most of the blessings that come through me, come through the imperfect. It is through our mistakes, our misses, our almosts, that we bless the lives of others. All of that mess belongs. There exists, as William James called it, an "unseen order" in my disorder.

What a relief. Still, it's hard to *feel* that relief when someone points out my flaws at work, not just because I have so many, but because I so want to be perfect. I have a constant need to prove that I'm not flawed because deep down, that's how I felt through most of my childhood. I was one big fat mistake. There's a core of that leftover shame inside me that gets activated now and then when someone criticizes my work. There's still a lingering belief that when I make a mistake, I am a mistake. Not just what I did is flawed, but who I am is one big flaw.

I've always loved that one of my daughter's blue eyes has three brown stripes running through it. She always colored in those stripes in every drawing of herself. She never saw them as a flaw, but as a unique imprint God had left on her alone. If only we could see our flaws that way, as something beautiful and useful.

The potter reminded me that on everything we create there are two imprints: ours and God's. Both are good. Both belong.

If you're going to doubt anything, doubt your doubts.

A college professor once gave me a short, simple prayer to help conquer fear:

"Lord, I take refuge in You from cowardice."

Those are the words Zeki Saritoprak uses to silence his fears. He's a professor of Islamic studies at John Carroll University in Cleveland, where I got my master's degree in religious studies.

Most of us don't call ourselves cowards, and yet we constantly doubt ourselves instead of our doubts. I used to think being brave meant having no fear. When I heard this definition, I laughed out loud: *Bravery is being the only one who knows you're afraid.*

We're all just faking courage. Some of us just do it better than others. "Fake it till you make it" has carried me along for years. My friend Vicki taught me one better: "Faith it till you make it." That will carry me along forever.

Many years ago, I met a mom outside a church hall in Wadsworth, Ohio. She told me about her daughter, Diana, who wanted to be a writer. This mom was so proud of her daughter for knowing what she wanted to do with her life. Her face lit up when she talked about how Diana was always writing in journals, how she worked on her high school yearbook and got a story printed in the local paper.

But she said everyone was discouraging her daughter from pursuing what she loved. I heard the same discouraging words when I started my career:

There are no jobs in journalism, people told me.

There is no money in writing, they warned.

There is no room in the world for your voice, they challenged.

If I would have listened to all their doubts—and mine—I never would have ended up working nearly three decades as a professional journalist. I remember how worried I felt when I heard people tell me: Don't become a writer, you'll never be able to pay the rent. Don't become a writer, newspapers are a dying industry. Don't become a writer, the world already has too many.

It was hard not to listen. What did I know? I was a single mom who was broke and years behind my peers. They graduated from college at 21; I graduated at 30. I had more desire than actual talent, so I simply listened to the desire and let it rule me.

It was hard because my doubts often shouted down my desire.

Who do you think you are?

Who are you to dream so big?

Who cares about what you have to say?

The road was rocky at first. My first job barely covered the rent. All along, people kept warning me that newspapers were dying. They told me that in the 1980s when afternoon papers were folding across the country. They're telling me that now as digital news replaces print news. No one knows for sure what lies ahead.

The same kinds of people who cautioned me were older and wiser than me and made me fearful of my career choice. They understood the economy, the laws of supply and demand, the complexities of the job market and global economy.

So what.

I had to do what was in my heart, and they didn't know what that was. No one else really knows what's in our hearts but us. No one knows how loud your own heart sings or pines or aches to do what it alone loves.

There are scores of others out there like me. Not all of them want to be writers. Some want to be painters or architects or carpenters or dentists or undertakers. Someone out there is discouraging them or has already discouraged them from going after their hearts' desires.

I knew a man who wanted to be a funeral director with all his heart but got stuck taking over the family grocery business, until decades later when he broke free and became an undertaker. I worked for a funeral director who wanted to be a jazz musician but, to his dismay, spent his life running the family mortuary business. He never broke free of it.

Diana's mom told me she had wanted to be an artist but ended up studying chemistry and hated it. Finally, when she hit middle age, she went back to school and started working as a draftsman. She loves it.

You can't listen to the critics. The world is full of them. My guess is the critics are the same people who didn't go after their own dreams and feel that pain every time someone else goes after a dream.

There's room in the world for your desire, whatever it is. Someone out there needs your gift. There is room in the world for your voice. Someone out there needs to hear it. I finally told myself, *Writing is like music*. There can never be too many songs. Someone out there who hates country music loves rap, and vice versa. The person who is moved by Shakespeare may hate John Grisham. The readers who hate my voice may love yours.

People will tell you the world is full of writers, but most of them talk away their words, talk away the plots of their unwritten novels while downing shots at a bar because they're too afraid to risk failing. They embrace their doubts instead of going after their dreams.

To go after what you want in life, you have to silence the critics, starting with the biggest one: you.

Sometimes the job you want is the job you already have.

The day I was hired to work at the *Beacon Journal*, I cried the whole way home. An hour's worth of tears. Buckets.

Why? I had just accepted a job to be a business reporter. I hated business news. What if I had just made a horrible mistake? After six months of writing sales and earnings reports, I did get bored and restless. A local magazine offered me a job as a feature writer. One wise soul in the newsroom encouraged me to stay put to build a résumé, pension, and life experience.

"You've only been here a few months," he said. "Give this newsroom a chance. Give yourself a chance here. You'll never regret it."

He was right. That "boring" beat they gave me? It was a mix of leftovers no one wanted: farming, health insurance, and the blimp. This is how boring it was:

So I'm flying the Goodyear Blimp...

What?!

Yep.

I proposed a story to follow the Goodyear Blimp with a photographer. We drove from Akron to South Bend, Indiana, and I got to fly in the blimp while it was covering a Notre Dame football game. I spent days interviewing the rope crew, the guys on the ground, who are an amazing bunch. They don't get the glory of the pilots, but they greet the townspeople in the area and make them feel welcome when they line up to see the blimp.

There's nothing like riding in the blimp. It doesn't feel like flying. It feels like riding in a boat. You sort of bob along on the sky. It's uplifting but noisy. The TV camera crew took the door out to shove in a big camera to cover the game. It was so noisy we had to wear headphones. We were flying over Notre Dame, waving to Touchdown Jesus, the Golden Dome, watching the Fighting Irish against Michigan State. At halftime, the pilot turned to me and said, "Here, you drive."

Me? Me at the controls of the *Spirit of Akron*?

Whoa.

How could I say no? I was still pinching myself that I got to fly in the Goodyear Blimp. It's a rare treat usually reserved for corporate bigwigs who are the best clients of the tire company.

Flying it? WOW.

He explained how simple it was and pointed to two gauges. An altimeter with numbers and a dial that was split across the middle. The top half was blue. "That's for sky. Keep it in sky," he said. He warned me not to let the needle on the altimeter rise too much or the blimp would float up and the skin would get hotter and expand. He also told me to keep the blimp in the blue part. Don't let it head south to the ground.

No problem. How hard could it be?

I was doing great. Then he left to go to the bathroom. Yep. There is a bathroom on the blimp. Sort of. There's no toilet, just a tube. The fluid just "dissipates" into the atmosphere. At least that's what the pilot told me. (Tip: Never stand directly under the Goodyear Blimp.)

He walked down the gondola to the back of the blimp and I was alone at the controls. It was halftime. I was watching the band when all of a sudden, the altimeter needle jumped. So I pointed the blimp down, just a tad. The needle rose higher, so I pointed the blimp down more. The front of the blimp gondola is all window, so I was looking at the ground and bracing my feet so I wouldn't fall through the glass. Yikes! The blimp was no longer in the blue.

From the ground, it must have looked like a scene from a disaster movie with the blimp preparing for a crash landing on the 50-yard line. The pilot had to hold on to the seats as he walked back to me and grabbed the controls. He righted the blimp and said, "It's hard enough to use that thing without standing on your head." He also promised I would never, ever fly another blimp.

What an experience—at a job I thought I would hate.

That job gave me many opportunities far beyond covering business news once I decided to raise the bar for myself. I volunteered to go to El Salvador to write about the end of the war through the eyes of a boy who had lost his leg and got a prosthetic leg in Ohio. I flew to Northern Ireland to write about "the troubles" through the perspectives of children who came to America for the summer to escape them.

The secret to any job isn't to leave when you get bored or restless or irritable, but to stay and make it better. Sometimes we simply need to stay put and call it holy ground. A dear friend of mine used to change jobs every six months. She always ended up hating every job. Her solution was the geographic cure. The only problem was, she always took herself along. We all know people like that. The solution to every problem is to move. Moving will solve their marital woes, their drinking problem, their employment dilemma, their financial mess, their lack of passion, their surplus of boredom. A better solution is to change you, not the job. When you change you, the job automatically changes.

Moving might be the solution for some, but as the old story goes, the new guy in town asks an old-timer, "What are the people like in this town?" The old-timer asks, "What were they like in the last town?" The man says, "Mean and nasty." The old-timer answers, "Then that's what you'll find here." The next day, another new resident walks into the bar and asks what the people in this town are like. The old-timer asks, "What were they like in the last town?" The man says, "They were kindhearted and giving." The old-timer tells him, "Then that's what you'll find here."

You attract what you are. Or as Mr. Brady, father of the infamous Brady Bunch, once said, "Wherever you go, there you are."

The simple idea of staying put was transformed into a sacred vow by the monks of old. Saint Benedict had the idea of making a commitment to remain in one community to keep the monks from wandering off in search of the perfect place to serve God, as if such a place existed. The Trappist monk Thomas Merton struggled more with his vow of stability than his vow of poverty. He constantly fought the desire to leave the monastery for more solitude and a deeper experience of God. He ended up spending his life in a Kentucky monastery writing books about the holiness in the ordinary life around him.

You don't have to be a monk to figure out that the search for happiness takes place on the inner landscape, not in filling up a U-Haul every year. I have never lived outside of Ohio. My restlessness always found an outlet in changing the scenery of my workplace. I've been a journalist for nearly three decades. I went through phases and fads of wanting to leave for more money, more prestige, more fulfillment.

Maybe it's middle age that cries out, "Enough!" Or the not-so-subtle daily reminders that convince me to stay, like the postcard of the red ruby slippers my husband gave me. Dorothy's shoes remind me, "There's no place like home," and to not go searching for my heart's desire any farther than my own backyard.

I've heard reporters grumble—and I've been one of them—that if we were real writers, we'd be in New York City writing novels or for the *New York Times*. But one photographer I worked with, Robin Witek, showed me that we don't need to be anywhere but in the present moment to find fulfillment.

Her approach to life and to taking pictures was to choose a spot, wait, and let life happen around her. When she covered a basketball game, she didn't chase after the action, running up and down the court. She chose her spot and captured the action around her.

Once you choose a place to stay put in life, a job, or a town, the landscape will never fail to amaze you. No matter where you decide to sink your roots or grow your branches, you are already standing on holy ground.

Most of the time, the only person in your way is you.

I used to keep a yellow sticky note posted on my computer that read "Think like a man."

Men seemed to figure out how to get up the career ladder faster, earn more money at the top, and never complain about a glass ceiling or a sticky floor holding them back. I threw the sticky note away after the YWCA honored me with a Women of Achievement Award. The motto of the event was "A career ladder can be climbed in heels." I don't know about you, but I can't even walk in heels, much less climb a ladder in them.

Both women and men have given me a lot of tips for getting ahead. How do you climb up the ladder? You start by getting out of your own way. Some of us—insert my name here—come up with every form of excuse to avoid climbing over, under, or around the hurdles life throws at us.

We blame the boss, our dad, our seventh-grade teacher. We

blame the system; the economy; the people above us, below us, around us. We let all those buts get in our way. *Yeah, but this is the way we've always done it. Yeah, but the boss will never allow it. Yeah, but the board won't approve of it. Yeah, but I'm too old…too young…too inexperienced…too overqualified…too unskilled.*

It's time to get rid of your big but.

I have an entire excuse catalog for things I'm too scared to do or don't really want to do. Most of them start with the words *I can't*.

I can't; I'm too busy, too tired, too overwhelmed. I can't use LinkedIn, Facebook, Twitter, Excel, PowerPoint; it's too confusing and difficult. I can't; I'm not good with money, statistics, numbers, technology, machinery. I can't; I'm not smart enough to figure it out by myself and I'll do it all wrong.

Then there's the mysterious "they." "They" won't let me. Who exactly are we talking about?

Someone once told me, "If you don't want to do it, you'll find an excuse. If you want to do it, you'll find a way." It really is that simple.

We all know people who spend 15 minutes explaining why they can't do a task because they didn't have the time, yet the task would have taken 10 minutes less to complete than giving the excuse. I've been that person. I either didn't want to do the task or feared I'd do it wrong, so I didn't do it. My husband loves to remind me that I once said I'd never use e-mail. I resisted technology because I hated feeling powerless when it didn't work. My husband always tells me that when you're complaining or defending, you're losing. I finally stopped complaining and defending my weaknesses. Instead,

I learned how to embrace technology to empower me. I now love the freedom e-mail gives me to work from home. I once hated Facebook and Twitter until I hired someone to teach me how to use them.

We often hold ourselves back simply by believing we're being held back. My friend Michael used to tell me if you tie up a donkey long enough, once you untie him he'll stay there. You can get so used to being stuck you don't move once you're free.

What's keeping you stuck? It might not be a glass ceiling or a sticky floor. Usually it's the person standing between them: you. There's usually a payoff for being stuck. If you can blame someone else, you never have to be responsible for anything that goes wrong. The flip side is, nothing ever changes to improve your life.

I'm constantly amazed by people who refuse to excuse themselves from life. Victor Riesel was a newspaper columnist who keeps me from making excuses. I never met him, but I saved his obituary and read it often.

He was a syndicated labor columnist who wrote about corruption by gangsters and labor unions. One day he stepped out of a restaurant in Manhattan and a man threw acid in his face. Victor was blinded for life. His career could have ended that night back in 1956. But the person who wanted to silence him only made his voice stronger. Victor kept writing and typing his own columns. He woke early and his wife read the paper to him cover to cover before he went to the office. When he was attacked, his column was in 193 papers. Before he retired in 1990, it was in 350 papers.

Gee, how can I call in sick after reading that? How can I

whine about anyone holding me back? How can I complain about work conditions?

I can't.

I've known parents who banned the word *can't* from their kids' vocabulary. Strike it from your own. That's the first step in getting out of your own way. Here are a few more:

Preserve your power. Live a blame-free, no-fault, victim-free life. No one can make you feel or think or do anything that isn't right for you.

If you can't change a person, place, situation, or institution, change how you think, feel, or respond to it.

My friend Bob used to tell me, "If life stinks, check your own diaper first." It might not be the boss or a coworker who messed up. You could be sitting in a mess of your own making, or it could simply be your attitude that stinks.

Be you, but be the best version of you. Like it or not, people make judgments about your age, education, credibility, and expertise based on midriff tops, low-cut blouses, miniskirts, tattoos, nose rings, and flip-flops. If you want to stand out in a memorable way, make sure it's how you want to be remembered.

Take the action you know to take. My friends in recovery love to tell the frog story: There are four frogs on a log. Three decide to jump off. How many are left on the log? Four. Those three only made a decision. They didn't take action. Take one small step that will propel you forward. Make the call. Send the e-mail. Ask for the raise.

Become teachable. It's hard for me to learn new things because I lack the humility to ask for help. Not knowing how to do something taps into that childhood core of shame inside me that tells me I'm stupid. I can now give myself permission to be a student of life. There is an endless supply of people to teach you anything you need to know. Pay them if you have to.

The best way to get out of your own way?

Take 100 percent responsibility for your own happiness and success. Stop believing that you're being held back. You can make an excuse or you can make it happen. It's always your call.

God is still speaking.

It's hard to imagine anyone willing to answer this old employment ad:

> We offer you no salary; no recompense; no holiday; no pensions, but much hard work; a poor dwelling; few consolations; many disappointments; frequent sickness; a violent or lonely death.

The job? Join the Sisters of the Presentation of the Blessed Virgin Mary.

As you might guess, nuns are a tough breed. The Dominican nuns taught me for eight years at Immaculate Conception School in Ravenna, Ohio. I never quite appreciated the contributions of nuns until I saw the national *Women & Spirit* museum exhibit that showed all they did to build schools, hospitals, and charities.

Catholic sisters created the country's largest private school system. They started some 110 universities. During the Civil War, they cared for both Union and Confederate soldiers. One nun started an insurance company for loggers so they'd have medical care coverage. Another one helped develop an incubator for newborns. One nun helped start the Mayo Clinic. Sister Henrietta Gorris, who helped rebuild poor neighborhoods after the race riots in Cleveland back in 1966, lived by a motto every inner city could use now: "Don't move, improve." One nun helped start Alcoholics Anonymous in Akron. Sister Mary Ignatia Gavin sneaked drunks into beds at St. Thomas Hospital to help them sober up.

And yes, some of them beat multiplication tables into us. I still have the scars on my knuckles. Even that was gently addressed. One exhibit stated: "Memories of Catholic school graduates vary widely, from affectionate to painful." I looked but didn't see a yardstick on display.

At every twist and turn of history, nuns helped and healed others. A giant cylinder bore the names of every order from Adorers of the Blood of Christ to Xavier Sisters. They changed the world not by force, but by prayer and a loyalty to their mission to serve others, a mission that constantly changed.

The nuns I had throughout grade school taught me how to read, write, add, subtract, and tell time. They also taught me that we might have more than one mission in life. I used to wonder what God's will was for me, used to struggle with finding out that one perfect thing God chose for me alone. What was my personal mission in life? The nuns taught me by their own lives that a person's mission in life might constantly change.

Sister Mary Ann Flannery used to be a college professor. Then she became director of the Jesuit Retreat House in Parma, which I call my spiritual home. She told me that the exciting thing about being a nun is: "You go where the grace leads you. You let the street be your chapel. You let your love of others be your vow." She's not boxed in by any one calling. She knows God is still speaking and listens daily for that day's direction.

The hardest part of being a nun, at least according to the ones I've talked to, isn't the vow of chastity. You don't hear scandals about nuns running amok and having affairs right and left. The hardest part is letting go of all they have loved about their sisterhood as convents merge and close. Nuns, I fear, are on the verge of extinction.

Nuns have taught me not to let the last word of God get in the way of the next word of God. God is still speaking. God's will might be one thing, or it might be many, or it might change as life changes. They constantly reinvent themselves as the inner evolution unfolds.

Sister Evangeline Doyle was my sixth-grade teacher. She did her best, but she didn't seem to love teaching a bunch of hormonally challenged boys and girls. I found out why when she stopped teaching.

She was an artist who felt like she was going to explode if she didn't create. She was small and frail but could attack a 5,000-pound chunk of limestone with a mallet and chisel like no one else. She traded in her habit for a pair of faded jeans and a torn sweatshirt. For years she was a hidden sculptor, making creations in the convent basement. She finally quit teaching and dedicated herself to her art. She stayed a nun but signed her work as Vang. She made endless paintings and sculptures in wood, limestone, and clay, including a massive one in front of the public library in Akron. Her goal was to help others appreciate the beauty in all things, to find God in everything.

I saved the prayer card from her funeral. It carried this quote by her: "There is a certain mystery of life in stone, it is so strong and enduring. Within the stone the artist comes into contact with the mystery of God's own creation."

I never got to thank her for showing me how to say yes to my dream. That's why it was important to thank my second-grade teacher. Sister Eleanor Wack didn't just teach us to read; she taught us to read the face of God. She taught us that God's face wasn't just in the man hanging on the crucifix, but in nature, in one another, and in every experience life would hand us.

When she shared her love of the stars with one class, a child stayed up late to see what the fuss was all about. The next day the breathless boy told her, "Sister, I saw Orion last night."

Sister Eleanor saw God everywhere, especially in the toothless grins of six-year-olds whose noses she wiped and whose shoes she tied. For 50 years, she taught hundreds to read Dick and Jane and Dr. Seuss. Adults came up to her in restaurants all over Akron to thank her for their love of reading.

She started her first day of teaching as Sister Dismas, back when I had her. She finished her last day as Sister Eleanor. At 74, her knees gave out. I went to say good-bye, and to thank her.

She was the last Dominican from Our Lady of the Elms in Akron to teach full-time. At one time the order had almost

220 sisters, nearly all of them teachers. She spent her last day hugging children, comforting weeping mothers, and greeting former students. A deputy chief from the Akron Police Department showed up to say good-bye. So did I. The report card she gave me in second grade says she taught me phonics, spelling, and arithmetic. It doesn't say that she taught me to love learning.

Back then, she was wrapped in a Dominican habit that revealed only her face and hands. They were enough. In those blue eyes and gentle hands, we caught more than a glimpse of how much God loved us.

The report cards her students glue in scrapbooks don't say that she taught them to say "Pardon me?" instead of "What?" or to spend at least four minutes in prayer every night—two minutes to talk to God and two minutes to listen.

"I try to teach them for life, to become what God planned them to be," she said.

After the children left, she took down the sign in room 109 that read SISTER ELEANOR'S ROOM.

"I'm not a crier, but in my heart I'm crying," she confided.

Before the final bell, she reviewed one last lesson. "What do you say when someone isn't nice to you?" she asked.

One boy recited, "You're not my friend, but I see God in you."

Sister smiled and told him, "That'll last you a lifetime."

It will. It did for me.

Make gentle the life of this world.

The Lost Boys of Sudan stood in the big medical supply warehouse early one morning waiting for the chance to send help back home.

At one point they broke into song, singing words in Dinka that had renewed their spirits back in 1983 when they were boys fleeing the civil war in Sudan. As children, they ran from bullets, crossed rivers infested with crocodiles, and walked thousands of miles under the blazing sun from Sudan to Ethiopia to Kenya.

As they sang in the MedWish International warehouse in Cleveland, one of them, Majier Deng, explained to me the song's meaning. "It's a God song," he said softly. "When we went from place to place, God always bless us, protect us, wherever we are, whatever we do."

Peter Manyiel nodded. "God helped us survive," he said.

"We always put everything in God hands. Today, we giving back."

The Lost Boys of Sudan are no longer lost and no longer boys. The six men sang to bless the medical supplies bound for South Sudan as a forklift hummed around them. Six of the Lost Boys came to help pack 10,000 pounds of medical supplies into a 40-foot-long cargo container bound for South Sudan. It is so poor there, one in seven children die before turning five. People walk two hours to a clinic or wait for help under a tree. There is no hospital, no equipment, no beds.

Majier said the shipment will show the people of Sudan that someone cares. "That is true love, to care about someone you don't know," he said.

Dr. Lee Ponsky started MedWish International in 1993 when he was just 20. He wanted to be a doctor and ended up working one summer at Mt. Sinai Hospital in Cleveland. He wanted to go somewhere else and make a difference. He has made it his life's mission to collect local medical supplies that would end up in landfills and send them to poor countries all over the world to save lives.

As a medical student working in a clinic in Nigeria, he saw doctors make their own saline, use fishing line for sutures, and run out of clean water during surgery. It was Lee's job to wash, powder, and sew up medical exam gloves to use again.

Lee graduated from the University of Rochester, and then he got his medical degree at Case Western Reserve University. He started the nonprofit MedWish in his parents' garage. He later became chief of urological oncology at University Hospitals in Cleveland.

He calls MedWish his hobby. Some hobby.

The Cleveland Clinic donates the use of the 38,000-square-foot warehouse that he has transformed into an international medical supply depot. MedWish collects and distributes medical supplies from 50 hospitals and nursing homes from Cleveland to California. MedWish ships to more than 90 countries, from Belize to Zambia. It takes no government funding and runs solely on donations.

It costs from $5,000 to $10,000 to ship one container. Each container is customized for what that country needs and what limitations it may have regarding clean water and electricity. MedWish vets every recipient. The containers are filled in Cleveland, put on a train, taken to a port city, and sent out by sea. MedWish helps deal with customs, impassable roads, changing political climates, and rules that vary from country to country. The organization is able to match good intentions with practical realities on the ground. MedWish tracks when the container arrives and when it is released.

People drop off walkers and wheelchairs, unopened gauze and gloves. Most donors prefer to be anonymous. One nursing home donated beds. A hospital donated sleep sacks for babies and burn dressings. The warehouse is full of hospital beds, incubators, operating room lights, mattresses, examination tables, IV poles, infant airways and bottles. There are stacks of beds, wheelchairs and dialysis machines, incubators and operating lights ready to go.

"Everything you see in this warehouse would be thrown in a landfill," Lee told me. "What we throw away is gold in other parts of the world."

I love the small sign attached to the office refrigerator: THE

Person Who Says It Cannot Be Done Should Not Interrupt the Person Doing It. MedWish runs with the help of donors, volunteers, and special-needs students paid to sort items.

Huge banners on the wall remind everyone of the mission. Each shows the face of one child from Africa, Central America, the Middle East, and South America. When I met Dr. Ponsky, I thought of those powerful words by Robert F. Kennedy: "Let us dedicate ourselves to what the Greeks wrote so many years ago: to tame the savageness of man and make gentle the life of this world."

That's what Lee Ponsky is doing here. A manual resuscitator sent to Laos saved the lives of five babies. A defibrillator considered outdated by U.S. standards is saving lives in Gabon, Africa. A heart valve MedWish sent to Honduras saved the life of a 16-year-old girl. A group of 67 volunteers took supplies to Nicaragua that treated the back pain of poor farmers. The patient who came in with bad arthritis and a knee brace made of wilted cabbage leaves held together with rags left with an elastic band and a smile.

There's a map of the world and a large wipe board that reads "Currently shipping to: Honduras, Ghana, Nicaragua, Peru, Uganda." It lists the "hot items" needed most: gauze, gloves, antibiotic cream, tongue depressors, and stethoscopes.

If you're going on vacation, you can take a box of medical supplies with you and turn your vacation into a lifesaving medical mission. Doctors traveling overseas stop in and get supplies. One doctor visiting Vietnam filled his suitcase with nebulizers.

Donors can adopt a room: pediatric supplies, wound care,

maternal health care, sutures, instruments, IVs, personnel protection—gloves, masks, and the like. There are tubs of breathing tubes, infant airways, baby bottles, catheters, maternity pads, and suction devices. Maternal packs include everything midwives need to deliver a baby.

The Lost Boys smiled at the pallets of bandages, gauze, ointments, IV poles, exam tables, wheelchairs, stretchers, gurneys, beds, and mattresses headed for South Sudan. They walked past a wall with a map of the world full of stickpins where containers have gone, to Central and South America, Africa, and beyond. A map of Ohio bulges with stickpins showing where the volunteers come from.

"Thank you, thank you," the Lost Boys said, almost in song.

They wanted to tuck something else into the shipment. They sat at a table and wrote letters to put inside the cargo container. Slowly and carefully, they printed words of hope for people on the other side of the ocean.

"This gift from MedWish is just a beginning," Majier wrote. "Keep praying and trusting in God Almighty. This gift, I hope, will make a difference."

Lazarus Makhoi paused a moment, then wrote the words he had wanted to hear all those years ago when he was that boy in a refugee camp:

"I didn't forget about you."

To help make a difference, go to www.medwish.org.

Sometimes your mission is revealed moment by moment.

Life always gives us exactly what we need at every moment, and in every moment, we get the chance to bless life back.

There's a lovely quote by American Zen pioneer Charlotte Joko Beck that I keep on my desk to remind me that every bug, every problem, every traffic ticket, every boss, every bump, every bruise, every breath teaches us something. "Every moment is the guru," Joko Beck said.

In every moment lies your mission.

How long is a moment? I don't know, but I once heard that a minute is a moment with handles. It takes a mere 60 seconds to make a difference. Cancer taught me that.

The nurses and doctors who cared for me didn't have a lot of time to comfort me while they cared for me. They had other patients to juggle, but they took care to make every moment matter.

When I woke up from a surgical biopsy, the surgeon came to answer my questions. Right before Dr. Leonard Brzozowski left my bedside to check on the pathology report to see if the lump he had taken out of my breast was cancer, he did something I've never forgotten. He squeezed my toes. It was a small moment of human connection, but a powerful act of grace. I was wrapped in a surgical bra, tucked in a thin hospital gown, and wearing those little hospital socks. I felt so vulnerable. That little squeeze helped me trust him then and down the road, the day we shared a big moment.

The day he peeled off all the layers of gauze around my chest so I could see what I looked like for the first time after a double mastectomy, he sat next to me on the hospital bed and unwrapped me slowly and tenderly, as if opening a fragile gift. He created a sacred moment for me to see my new body. He did it in a way that put both me and my husband at ease with my blank chest.

Then there was the nurse who called me at home after surgery. She said she wanted to check in on me to see how I was doing. It might have been a routine call, but she did it with compassion that I could feel through the phone. She told me she was sorry I had to go through cancer.

In my work and in my time as a patient and as an EMT, I've talked to nurses from recovery rooms, coronary care, pediatrics, geriatrics, and ER and trauma units. They've shared the comedy and tragedy of the job, how they're pushed and pulled in 100 ways, how they barely get a chance to use the bathroom, how they end up wearing blood and vomit home.

Nurses are the patient's advocate, the doctor's eyes and ears, and everyone's scapegoat. They can page your doctor but can't make the doctor magically appear. My sister is a nurse and wears a T-shirt around the house that reads "Be kind to nurses. We keep doctors from accidentally killing you."

What do they get in return? They're greeted with "Hey you...Yo...Lady...Nurse Ratched" and choice words they're too kind to repeat. They also are called IV leaguers and the heartbeat of health care. The few times in my life when I've had the misfortune to be a patient, nurses came through for me.

I wasn't always a compliant patient 16 years ago when I was diagnosed with breast cancer. When it came time to set up my chemo appointments, I wanted to schedule them around my volleyball games. I hadn't yet wrapped my brain around the concept that I had a life-threatening disease. I kept trying to delay setting up the chemo because I was scared. Finally the nurse looked at me and said firmly, "You need to get your priorities straight." I threw a fit and demanded a new nurse, but deep down, I knew she was right.

When the antinausea drugs weren't working, my chemotherapy nurse, Pam Boone, spoke up for me and pestered the doctor for better medicine to put in my IV when I lacked the energy to speak up.

I met him only once, but a nurse named John in radiology called me honey and promised I would get through six weeks of daily radiation in no time, and I did.

Countless others, whose names I never knew, watched over me. Anonymous blurs in scrubs, those angels in comfortable shoes left behind an imprint of compassion in the squeeze of a hand, the caress of a cheek, the fluff of a pillow.

Nurses are up there with grandparents and guardian angels.

They are dedicated to the weak, the confused, the broken of body, mind, and spirit. They don't care if you throw up on them, miss the bedpan, or hit the call light in the middle of the night just because you're scared and don't want to be alone. They will go to bat for you against disease, track down doctors on golf courses, and stay late just to check on you one last time. And they do it all, minute by precious minute.

Oh, the things they put up with. The fights from the Jerry Springer families who smuggle in beer and bring diabetics doughnuts, then demand more insulin and threaten to sue if they don't get it. They mistake a hospital for a hotel and the nurse for a housekeeper.

Nurses get yelled at, kicked, slapped, punched, spit on, and sexually harassed by people in various states of mental illness, intoxication, and just plain arrogance. The paycheck doesn't begin to cover the endless miles nurses walk, the meals they skip, the holidays they miss with their families. They stay on their feet for 12-hour stretches to wash blood and glass off a car crash survivor, stabilize a broken neck, teach a mother to nurse a newborn, save a diabetic's leg, help a hospice patient let go.

Nurses have told me about family members who have started fights, untied restrained patients, poked around gunshot wounds, brought in babies and let them crawl on the floor, ordered pizzas and left the mess behind.

People don't go into nursing because they love the paperwork or the pain-in-the-neck patients, families, and doctors. They go into nursing because they want to help people. It isn't a job. It's a calling. A minute-by-minute, moment-by-moment calling.

Nurses have taught me that it takes only a moment to make a difference, to make the mother of a newborn feel celebrated and the mother of a stillborn feel comforted.

It takes only a moment to help the homeless and lonely feel at home in the world. To make a teenager with cancer feel confident she can face her classmates bald at the senior prom. To give senior citizens their dignity when they have to use a bedpan, a catheter, or a diaper.

It takes only a moment to make a woman who just lost both breasts believe she is still whole. To make a stroke patient who can no longer speak feel understood. To dry some tears, hold a hand, or tell a son that his mother forgave him before she took her last breath.

Nurses help newborns take their first breaths and grandparents take their last. In between those bookend breaths, nurses make scared children feel safe and scarred people feel beautiful. They fulfill their calling in life every time they answer a call light.

They constantly remind me that each of us can be the light, even if all we do is shine for a moment.

When things fall apart, they could actually be falling into place.

There's an old saying: "Some years ask questions, some years answer them." Most of us would rather be living in a year with answers.

Sometimes you go through months or years of uncertainty, where everything on the outside looks stagnant. You're stuck in a winter where you can't see the growth. When you look back on those periods of time, you were growing roots.

Some years you see the fruits of your labor, you flower, you bloom, you strut your stuff, and the world sees a bouquet and celebrates. Root years aren't so attractive. There's not much to show for them until much later in your life when you realize that those were the most vital years of all.

I thought of that when I heard about Mary Ann Corrigan-Davis. She had a dream job, then lost it and found a more perfect dream. She graduated from college with a degree in

French and planned to go into international business. She got her MBA from Case Western Reserve University and expected to get the perfect job in international business as soon as she graduated.

It took a year of interviews to find a job, and when she did, it was in sales at American Greetings, the card company. She planned to stay briefly and then move on to pursue her dream job. She stayed for 27 years. She ended up as president of the Retail Division in charge of 440 stores across 40 states, worked in Australia, and climbed the ladder all the way to the rung called Senior Vice President of Business Innovation. Then it all came to a screeching halt.

She got downsized. Then her dad died. Then she got breast cancer.

All in one year.

She said, "Lord, You have my attention. What is it You would like me to do?"

It looked muddy and messy at the time, but looking back, it's clear what that time was for.

She got to be with her dad in his final days.

She got to heal and make getting well her full-time job.

She got to strengthen her faith when she went through chemotherapy and radiation, a faith that was deepened by her years at Saint Joseph Academy, an all-girls Catholic high school.

After Mary Ann survived the storm, she found a huge rainbow. She ended up in the job of her dreams, one that didn't exist until she got downsized. She's now president of Saint Joseph Academy, the school she always loved. She likes being in a workplace driven by a sense of mission, not profit.

"Life is like a roller coaster," she told me. "Sometimes you do want to throw up. You just have to believe it will get better."

How do you keep believing?

You make denial work for you. You believe in spite of the statistics. You believe past your doubts. You believe anyway.

When I was diagnosed with cancer in 1998, once I got past the fear, cancer seemed like such a big waste of time. I was practically useless as far as work was concerned. Or so it seemed. I spent endless hours at doctor's appointments and medical procedures. Everyone else was busy completing to-do lists and conquering the world, and I was conquering the next MRI, CAT scan, or side effect from chemo.

Cancer sucks. There's no polite way of saying it. Cancer sucks away your energy and enthusiasm. Even when you feel good, you don't yet feel normal. It's like having the flu for a year. Cancer put me in the slow lane of life. A lane I resented at the time but am grateful for today. The whole cancer experience deepened every area of my life and forced me to grow spiritually, emotionally, and physically. I always wanted to be able to inspire people to live their best lives. So much of what inspires me came from that slow lane I traveled in. The slow lane of life teaches you to do what is necessary, then do what is possible, and pretty soon, you're doing the impossible.

It was a scary time. In my family, cancer was fatal. Everyone who got it before me had died. My aunts Veronica, Francie, and Maureen all died from breast cancer. I got breast cancer at 41. A year later, two cousins were diagnosed with it. That's when we all decided to get genetic testing.

I found out I carry a mutation called BRCA1. It raises the

lifetime chance of getting breast cancer to 85 percent. Five of my cousins have been diagnosed with breast cancer. My sister Patricia was tested for the gene. She had it and decided to do something about it.

She tells everyone, "I cheated cancer."

Boy, did she.

With courage and grace and grit.

She's the youngest girl in our family of 11. She remembers going with my dad to visit his sister Veronica in the hospital when she was fighting cancer. He brought her wigs. Veronica died at 44, leaving behind six children, ages 2 to 14.

Patricia decided to be proactive and not wait for cancer to show up. She had a preventive bilateral mastectomy with reconstruction at the age of 39. Her son was just 2.

Then we found out my daughter carried the gene. I had passed it on to her. Oh, the sadness over giving her a gene that could threaten her life. And yet having that gene changed her life and shaped it.

A year after she found out that she carried the BRCA1 gene, Gabrielle started a job at University Hospitals working with the National Cancer Institute. She had been working in human resources and saw the job ad. It sounded like the perfect fit. As partnership program coordinator for NCI's Cancer Information Service, she worked with organizations to share the latest cancer information and help people learn about lifestyle changes, screening, and clinical trials to reduce their cancer risk and increase their survival odds. Part of her job was to make cancer information and treatment available to those who didn't have insurance. She was saving lives.

When she couldn't find a support group for young women

with the gene, she helped start one. She connected with other women in online support groups for "previvors," women who haven't had breast cancer but have the gene for it. Having the breast cancer gene both scared and empowered her. Educating others gave her a sense of control over what she couldn't control. She looked out for the family. She collected everyone's diagnosis and surgery history to put into a family tree to pass along to all cousins. She became our family's personal educator and sent us the latest on studies, conferences, clinical trials, and online resources.

She, too, had both of her breasts removed. It was sad at first, but now that she's the mother of three, she's just grateful every day to be alive to see them grow up. Once she had children, she decided to quit her job and become the full-time CEO of her home. She's never been happier.

Another gift came out of all this. Back when I was looking for a dress to wear to my daughter's wedding, it was hard to find something elegant that wasn't strapless or low cut. The dress had to hide the thick industrial-sized straps on my mastectomy bra that holds my prosthetic breasts. Other survivors had told me to make friends with my new bosom buddies, so I named them Thelma and Louise. Patricia helped me look for a mother-of-the-bride dress and was struck by how hard it was to find the right clothes after having a mastectomy.

Then, when my daughter had to make peace with her surgery and sadness over having to wear mastectomy swimsuits for the rest of her life, Patricia got to work. She pulled out her sketchbook and began to draw swimsuits. My sister the architect started to design luxury swimwear for women who have had mastectomies. She named her line of suits Veronica

Brett, in honor of our aunt. Patricia wants every woman to feel beautiful and elegant and special. I love how I feel and look in her suits.

The tagline on her swimsuits is a perfect fit for the suits and for anyone facing the changes ahead with courage: "LIFE NEVER LOOKED SEXIER."

When you fail, fail forward.

My husband is a perfect failure.

He's great at falling down. He's even better at bouncing back up.

Before we met, he had many different careers. He came to the marriage with a good solid résumé of failures behind him.

He was always an entrepreneur. In high school, he made and sold bumper stickers and buttons with messages of love and peace.

He tried other things. He worked at a steel factory. For one whole day. The foreman handed him a hard hat and told him to go empty that truck and pointed to the biggest tractor trailer Bruce had ever seen. It was full of boxes of aluminum siding. They were so long, the boxes bent in the middle when he lifted them. It was 120 degrees in the shade. It took all day. At the end of that day, Bruce handed the foreman his hard hat. "This isn't for me," he said.

He spent a summer working in a catalog showroom near home. The manager looked at him and said, "You're the only kid in the neighborhood I'm gonna hire. You're the only kid whose father didn't call ahead. You walked in on your own." Bruce never forgot that lesson.

He went to college, got married at 20 to a woman whose dad owned a jewelry store. Bruce took over the costume jewelry side of the business. For seven years. He hated every minute of it, but he learned how to sell. He liked owning a business, he just didn't like that business.

"I learned how to take pleasure in the margins," he said. "I found an avocation."

He had a flair for organizing and getting involved in local politics. He ran a huge street fair attended by 60,000 people. He filmed a documentary on it for the local cable access channel.

But he was paralyzed when it came to changing jobs. It wasn't until his hand was forced that he took action, when interest rates went up to 20 percent and inflation skyrocketed. No one was paying him what they owed and his suppliers demanded cash. He took a second mortgage on his house to get out of debt. One day he saw an ad in the paper for an executive director of a large Jewish synagogue and applied. He was only 27 and knew nothing about running a 1,200-family synagogue, but he had learned how to recruit and use volunteers at the street fair, and he had balanced books for his jewelry business. Somehow he got hired.

The first year, he was so lost he felt like he was in an aquarium. He could see people talking but couldn't understand a word they were saying. He oversaw 15 employees, 25 active committees, 2 cemeteries, and a catering operation. He lasted three years. Then one day the president fired him. The board rehired him, but he knew it was time to move on.

Bruce had been selling the remaining inventory of his costume jewelry business on the weekends at flea markets and to retail stores trying to cover his second mortgage until the phone rang and his mother-in-law said, "Come to work right away. Your business is gone."

All that costume jewelry inventory he kept in the basement of his father-in-law's store? A water main broke and the basement flooded. Eight feet deep. The jewelry fell apart. Bruce lost everything. He still remembers the stench and mud and mold. He lost thousands of pieces of jewelry. The insurance company offered 50 cents on the dollar. "If you don't like it, sue us," they said. Bruce had no money to sue. He took the money.

He went on to sell car phones, which back then were used only by the wealthy. They cost over a thousand dollars each. He was salesman of the month for three months. The fourth month, he missed his quota. The next month he missed it again and got fired.

He's never forgotten that day when he was standing at a pay phone with tears running down his face and he had to call his wife and tell her, "I got fired." They had two kids and no income.

Bruce ended up doing public relations and property rezonings for a chain of car dealerships. Then, one day, he took his biggest gamble and opened his own public relations business. He starved for six months, maxed out two credit cards, and took out a third to borrow money to make the minimum payments on the first two cards. He was $25,000 in debt and terrified. His wife kept saying, "Just get a job." But he didn't want a low-paying job. He wanted to be the man who signed the front of the check, not the back. The business grew. He got a partner, and it grew more. Then he got divorced, which felt like a failure.

Two years later, he met me.

When I met my husband, he owned the small public relations firm, which specialized in everything. He did it all, from political campaigns to rezoning issues. He made a great living until the terrorist attacks of September 11. Those attacks scared business owners all over the country, and they trimmed any nonessential costs out of fear. The phone stopped ringing at my husband's firm. Business evaporated. For six months, he didn't have one billable hour. He lost so many clients, he lost the business. He had to shut the doors.

He came home that last day of work beaten down like a whipped dog. While he was emptying his office, my daughter and I turned a spare bedroom into an office for him. He would need to remake himself in time. I figured he'd look for a job. A few weeks later, he announced he was ready to start another business. Was he crazy?

He wanted to use our home equity line to fund it. Was he crazy?

After much prayer and counsel with friends and confronting my own fears, I agreed. Was I crazy?

A good friend, Bob Smith, CEO of the large investment firm Spero-Smith, told Bruce to quit trying to be all things to all people and focus his business in one area. For years, Bruce had lurched from project to project with no plan. Bruce decided to make this time the last time. What were his skills? What did he love? Crisis communications. That would be his brand. It sent his adrenaline rushing. He would choose one thing, go narrow and deep, and do it better than anyone.

For a few months I paid all the bills and trusted all would be well. Within two years, he had paid back all the money. Within five years, he was earning more than he had before and still worked out of that bedroom office. He got a new partner and renamed the business Hennes Paynter Communications. By year ten, the company had grown so big that they moved the business out of their homes to downtown Cleveland on the 32nd floor of Terminal Tower, the heart of Cleveland.

The year the economy was the worst, they had their best year. They created a business that is recession-proof. They have clients all over the country.

"I love what I do," he tells people. "I haven't worked a day in thirteen years." That doesn't mean he doesn't work hard. He works harder than anyone I know. Some would say too hard. (Me.)

A mystic named Julian of Norwich said, "First there is the fall, and then we recover from the fall. Both are the mercy of God." Or as my friend Bob always says, "I fall and I rise up. Both are the grace of God."

He's right. Failure can be your best teacher. If your life looks like a mess, it could be because you're still in the middle of it. The middle always looks messy. It's simply too soon to tell how it will all turn out. It turned out better than Bruce ever imagined.

"Every person I met, every job I held, every sale I ever

made, every experience I ever had, gave me the happiness and success I have today," Bruce said.

The benefits of failure are endless. Failure strips away fear. Once you've failed, you have nothing left to lose. You realize that you're still alive, still breathing, still you, and life goes on. When you strip your life down to survival mode, you realize you don't need all that much to survive or to serve others. You discover what you're truly made of, and that you're tougher than you ever knew.

Choice, not just chance, determines your destiny.

How do you make the right choice to take a new job or to stay where you are, to choose one college over another, to choose one calling over another?

It's easy to decide when one choice is obviously good and one is clearly bad. It's tough to choose when both options appear equally good or bad.

I had been working at the *Beacon Journal* in Akron, Ohio, for 14 years. During that time, I got married and moved to Cleveland. My life was no longer centered in the Akron area. When you're a newspaper columnist, it's important to live near the people you write about to capture the feeling of the city. It was time to get my life in one place.

I approached the *Plain Dealer* in Cleveland and they offered me a job as a columnist. Should I take it? To make it more complicated, the editor at the *Beacon Journal* found out and offered me more money to stay than the *Plain Dealer* had offered me to leave.

What should I do?

There's no secret formula, no one-strategy-fits-all solution to use to make decisions. Or maybe there's a different one for everybody.

There's the easy way out. I could turn over a Magic 8 Ball and ask again later, consult my horoscope, throw darts at a board, flip a coin, or play Bible bingo. That's where you open the Good Book, point a finger to any random passage, and—voilà!—there's the answer.

There's the old standby: write down the pros and cons of each choice and go with the longest "pros" list.

Another option is to pick the two best choices and try them on for a day like a pair of new shoes to see how they fit. Let's say you want to move to Kalamazoo or Chicago. You choose one city and imagine living in it for one day. You pay attention to how it feels in your head, heart, and gut. The next day, you try on the other choice. Usually by noon of the second day, you know which to choose.

I've heard that it helps to separate fact from fiction. Once you've done that, discard the fiction. Once you have all the facts, separate the relevant facts from the irrelevant ones. Base decisions on those alone. Don't assume anything. As one journalism teacher taught me, any time you assume, you might make an *ass* of *u* and *me*.

My friends in recovery taught me to apply the Four Absolutes of Alcoholics Anonymous: honesty, purity, unselfishness, and love. They ask themselves these questions when confronted with a choice: Is it true or is it false? Is it right or wrong? How will this affect the other person involved? Is it ugly or beautiful?

You could just take a shower. Seriously. Sometimes your subconscious will take over and hand you the solution.

Or take a poll. Consult your inner circle of friends. Form your own board of directors of people whom you respect most and run the decision by them.

You could just let fate decide for you. "It is what it is," people say all the time. They don't realize that not deciding is a decision.

What I try to do most often is move from the outer methods of choosing to the inner ones. The priests I met at the Jesuit Retreat House in Cleveland shared a formula they learned from Saint Ignatius of Loyola, who started their religious order. They suspend all fear, anxiety, and doubt and stay focused on their mission to praise and serve God. They make themselves indifferent to health, wealth, fame, and longevity. They desire and choose only what will help them be of the utmost service to God and others.

I like the idea of thoughtful discernment. To consciously ask for clarity and then wait for it. You usually have to wait until the noise clears. Some days it feels like recess at a day care in my head, with so many toddlers running around in so many different directions.

The key is to discern which voice is God's and which one isn't. One priest described the Holy Spirit speaking the way water falls gently on a sponge, while what isn't God comes to us like water pounding violently on rocks. The voice that isn't God becomes easier to recognize over time. For me, it's the noise and static inside that makes me feel sad, guilty, or confused. The voice that makes me feel weighed down by life, or restless and irritable, isn't God's voice. Confusion, noise, and frustration are my three signs to stop ruminating. My friend Ruth often reminds me, "Don't believe everything you think." I need to wait for the quiet, clarity, and peace to catch up. Sometimes I actually hold up my hand and yell, "Stop!" and the noise does.

When I'm feeling beat up from within, it isn't God holding the club, it's me. My God isn't armed. My God is a loving, joyful, gentle God. The clarity of God's love comes to me through a calm peace that creates either an opening or a closing. Then, no matter what I choose, I confirm it with the people I trust the most: my husband, children, and closest friends.

When I feel lost, I've learned to wait it out. The confusion and doubt will pass, like turbulence on a plane. I might be in for a bumpy ride, but I stay the course. I can't let noisy passengers be my guide. The best thing for me is to wait. I don't make any changes until the clarity comes. I pray for clarity, then meditate to receive it. I've learned not to make any decision under the influence of despair or fear or fatigue.

I'm not saying that you should do nothing while you wait. Keep praying, meditating, journaling, talking to those who have your best interests at heart. Naps help, too. Sometimes, just before I rest, I pray for a spiritual awakening. As they say, the answer will always come—if you want it.

The answer came to me when I stopped wrestling with the decision. While struggling with whether to stay at the *Beacon Journal* or take the job at the *Plain Dealer*, I decided to stop thinking about it for 48 hours. I had done enough introspection and prayer. I had already asked for the clarity and inspiration. It was time to relax, take it easy, and trust that the answer would come when I was ready to hear it.

I drove four hours away to visit my daughter at college. We had a great weekend wandering around campus and shopping and laughing with her friends. As I packed up my things to leave, suddenly, I just knew. The answer came with total peace.

When I left that morning, I borrowed a blouse from her so I could drive straight to the *Beacon Journal* to break the news that I was leaving. I didn't know it, but my coworker and closest friend, Sheryl, who also had the chance to leave the *Beacon Journal* for the *Plain Dealer*, had made the same decision. Sheryl told our boss the same day I did. We even ended up wearing the exact same outfit to work: black slacks and a white blouse.

That sealed the deal.

And we've never looked back.

*It's not about what you can do, but what
God can do through you.*

Some days the bad news of the world can overwhelm you.

Poverty. Unemployment. Wars.

Who is going to fix everything that's wrong with the world?

Then you hear about guys like Rick Burns who decide to simply change their corner of it.

Burns Auto Service sits on a corner in a small town called Bay Village, Ohio. People bring in their cars for muffler repairs and oil changes, but one day, they started dropping off cash to help give one life a tune-up.

The sign outside Burns Auto Service advertises mufflers and tune-ups. The sign inside on the bulletin board tells what really happens here.

Rick Burns has curly hair the color of butterscotch candy. He wears blue work pants that look black from the oil and grease they absorb as he slides in, around, and under cars.

Rick's dad bought the gas station, then pulled out the pumps and made it a repair shop. Rick bought the shop from his dad ten years ago, right around the time Brian showed up.

Brian is 37 and lives with his mom. Most everyone in Bay Village knows him. They give him free haircuts at the barbershop and free coffee at the restaurants. Brian was born with cerebral palsy, which hampers his muscle control. Brian works at City Hall three days a week. He empties trash and stocks the bathrooms. City Hall is across the street from the auto shop, which is just a mile from his home.

Brian's world is small, but it's also deep because of people like Rick.

Brian used to sit in the front seat when his mom brought her car in for an oil change. That's how he met Rick.

Brian can't drive a car. He used to mope around the house. He started calling the auto shop for rides. Brian limps slowly. His body tilts to the left. He shuffles and drags his left foot. He keeps his left arm close to his side, where his hand lies curled up. It made Rick nervous every time he saw Brian cross the street, so one day, Rick placed an ad in the *Villager* newspaper:

Everyone in Bay Village knows Brian. Brian needs a good trike to get around town. Rick Burns of Burns Auto Service at Dover and Wolf roads wants to trick out a great new trike for Brian. Stop in at Burns Auto and make a donation for Brian's trike.

He didn't include a phone number, website, or address. He didn't need to.

People drove by and dropped off tens and twenties. In three weeks he raised $200.

Rick bought a cobalt-blue Schwinn three-wheel adult sports trike, a canopy to keep Brian out of the sun and rain, and a hundred dollars' worth of accessories. One lady dropped off a headlight. The police gave Brian an orange light stick and a pole with a reflective handicap logo on the top that spins. Someone gave him an American flag. Another person donated a reflector.

Jason Tuneberg, who works with Rick, put the bike together. It has headlights, taillights, front and rear brakes, a basket that folds down, tire valves that light up, a speedometer, racing pedals, and, of course, a bell.

"It's perfect for parades," Rick said.

Rick reached into the basket and held up a bike lock and key. "This is his security system," he said. "We keep the other key here in case we need to go save him."

The rearview mirror broke off.

"I hit the side of my garage," Brian confessed.

So far the fastest he has driven is eight miles per hour.

"I try not to go downhill," Brian said.

Inside the shop, repair orders are lined up neatly in a row on the counter. Rick has set toy trucks on a shelf at toddler eye level for children who have to wait with their parents. The bulletin board above is filled with news clippings of Cleveland Indians victories.

Rick pinned up the card Brian's mom sent thanking him for the bike. Underneath the card, a sheet of white paper with these typed words clarifies the mission of the auto shop. It isn't just a place to get mufflers and tune-ups.

Definition of Life: Life is not the number of breaths you take. Life is the number of moments that take your breath away.

"We got him out of the house," Rick said. "He's back on the road."

And back into life.

After I wrote a column about Rick, people filled envelopes with cash and shoved them through the key slot at Burns Auto. One anonymous donor gave $200. One man donated $100 and left a note asking Rick to buy a windshield and snow tires for Brian's bike. One man sent a big box with a bike helmet, gloves, radio, and a water bottle.

Everywhere Rick went, people said, "You're that guy." Women gave him hugs; men shook his hand. He collected $1,200. What would he do with the extra?

Then Jeannette drove up on her old trike, the one with the tires that go flat, the chain that falls off, the seat that wobbles without duct tape. Jeannette is a single parent with a son in high school and a daughter in third grade. Jeannette moves and talks slowly, enunciating words in her own unique way. She holds her hands behind her back and sways unless she needs her hands to sign words because she is hard of hearing. She's 41 and tells anyone she trusts that she was diagnosed with a developmental disability.

Jeannette rides a trike to get groceries, to go to the bank and the doctor. She can't drive a car because she has seizures. When she saw the trike Rick decked out for Brian, she started praying for one. God answered through Rick.

He bought her a trike like Brian's. He added a pink horn, headlight, pink tassels, radio, side mirror, two American flags, and a safety spinner. When he gave her the trike, she covered her face and started to cry.

Inside his shop he keeps a three-ring scrapbook with all the cards and letters people sent. One page is full of sticky notes on which he wrote down the gifts:

$50 Mrs. Camry

$50 walk-up lady

90-year-old man $100

Walgreens lady in line $20

$5 Dan landscaper

Rick took the lid off the blue coffee container on the counter. "Look at this," he said, pulling out a handful of bills. "The money is still coming in."

What's next?

Rick continues to give away new and used trikes that he and his team restore, paint, and customize. "I love doing it," he said. "We're blessed."

We all are, by people like him.

One evening I pulled into a parking lot and walked into the building where I was to give a speech and sign books. A woman stopped me and told me the back tire on my car was growing flat. Was it a slow leak or a fast one? What should I do? My talk would end around 9 p.m. By then it would be dark. As I stared at the tire, a man walked over and said, "Looks like you need help."

It was Rick. He just happened to come to my talk and just happened to have an air compressor in his trunk. He filled my tire and we went inside. After my talk, I found a note on my windshield. He had drawn a cross and written: "Your tire is fine. Check it tomorrow."

He took my breath away one more time when I opened the mail a few days later and found a box with this note: "Here's your own air compressor so you won't get stranded in the future. You might also be able to help someone else in need some day."

Instead of trying to be the best in the world,
be the best for the world.

What journalist doesn't want to win a Pulitzer Prize?

It's the greatest height a journalist can reach. Or so they say.

In my field, they tell you that once you win the Pulitzer, the first line of your obituary is already written.

I've come close to winning twice. Editors have nominated my work for the coveted prize many times, and I was actually chosen as a finalist twice.

The first time I was one of three finalists across the country for a Pulitzer Prize in commentary, I was giddy. I had written a series of 40 columns on inner-city violence. The judging is supposed to be a secret, but information often leaks out of who the three finalists are in each category. Two days before the winner was to be announced, I was sitting in a movie theater on a Saturday night when my editor called. I went out into the lobby to take the call. She told me I didn't win. I was crushed.

When I went to work that Monday, friends and coworkers didn't even try to console me. They were so excited and proud of me for being a finalist it didn't seem at all like I'd lost anything. They were right. It should have been enough, but my ego wanted more. My husband threw me a party. My friends, family, and coworkers gathered to celebrate that I was one of the top three columnists in the country that year, but deep inside I was disappointed that I wasn't Number One.

The second time, I was a finalist for columns I wrote that helped change the law in Ohio so prosecutors could no longer hide critical information from defense attorneys. For the category of commentary, you can submit up to ten columns, so we also sent columns I wrote about my daughter's decision to have a preventive double mastectomy at age 29. She inherited from me the BRCA1 gene for breast cancer, and sharing her journey was excruciating. I wanted to win for her, and, of course, for my ego.

I couldn't imagine losing this time.

But I did. This time, I found out in front of everyone in the newsroom as we gathered around to celebrate a victory as the Pulitzers were announced. Again, everyone said, "You didn't lose. You were a finalist!" They served cake and punch and everyone offered kind words. But I have this strange ego: If I don't win, I've failed. There's no middle ground. It's A or F. There are no other grades like B, C, or D.

The truth is, no prize can put that kind of ego to rest. Not even the Pulitzer Prize. My friend Bob, one of the greatest reporters in the business, won a Pulitzer Prize. It did nothing to silence his inner-doubt demons. Bob was always my personal monk in the newsroom. He often repeated to me a quote by

Bill Wilson, the founder of Alcoholics Anonymous, who said: "I had to be number one in all things because in my perverse heart I felt myself the least of God's creatures."

Bob helped me realize that once you become unattached to the world and its applause and don't depend on it for definition and affirmation, you're finally free to serve the world. Instead of trying to be the best in the world, be the best *for* the world.

One of his favorite sayings is: "I'd rather stand in the dark than in a light of my own making."

Can't I just stand in the light of the Pulitzer, too?

Deep down, I wanted to be famous, important, complimented, noticed, needed, respected, nurtured, praised. Every time I got some of that, it wasn't enough. Whenever I set a goal and reached it, I reached for another one that was out of reach. It was a chase for the horizon.

As much as I'd like to win a Pulitzer, the place that really means the most to me is under a refrigerator magnet. I'm honored that people cut out my columns and stick them on the fridge next to their son's A in science and their daughter's artwork. Readers open weathered wallets and unfold faded columns they'd tucked in there that touched them. A judge once called me into his chambers after a court hearing to show me the column of mine he kept under the glass on his desk. At one book signing, a woman brought a scrapbook of her little boy's life. I'd never met her, but I had seen her son's beautiful grin in a photo that ran on the obituary page when he died. I mentioned that smile and his name in a column and she never forgot. She asked me to sign that column she so carefully glued into her precious book about his brief life.

How humbling.

A quote from Isaiah 49 reminds me what truly matters: "I shall be glorious in the eyes of the Lord and my God shall be my strength." That's the glory I seek. When you are one with God, you don't have to prove your worth. I now aim to write for the greater glory of God, not for the greater glory of Regina.

Ego is a tricky thing. Some see it as a bad thing and call it **e**asing **G**od **o**ut. A coworker once told me ego isn't all bad if it motivates you to be of service. God might even find it useful. People with big egos can get a lot accomplished to help others. You can turn that famous Nike slogan into "Just Do It…for the glory of God." The key is, What's in it for God? I love Mother Teresa's answer to the person who said he couldn't do her job for a million dollars. She said she couldn't either. She did it for Jesus.

The goal isn't about being the best, but being the best for others. One reader never lets me forget the true worth of what I do. One year I was invited to a job fair for minorities at a prestigious law firm. I went and chatted with people there and wrote a column about some of the men and women looking for work. It wasn't a dazzling column. It wasn't great. I'm not even sure it was good. It definitely wasn't Pulitzer material. It was simply the best I could do with the material I had at the time.

It wasn't award-winning, but it turned out to be life-changing.

In the column, I mentioned that Tony Morrison, a commercial photographer, appreciated a chance to get a foot in the corporate door by attending the job fair. As a black man, he found it hard to break into the old established white guys' network, although he never used those words.

He expressed his gratitude for the job fair when I interviewed him. "You finally got past the receptionist," he said. "If you can show your product, you have a chance. It's like David against Goliath. By doing this they sort of leveled the playing field."

In a column of some 600 words, I used 50 to mention Tony.

Those 50 words changed his life. From that column on, he was hired all over town to take photos. Every year I see him at Cleveland's Chamber of Commerce Public Officials Reception where hundreds of movers and shakers gather to network. Tony is the official photographer, taking shots of senators, mayors, and CEOs.

Every year he comes up to me, sticks out his hand, and thanks me for his career.

And I thank him for reminding me about what matters most about mine.

If you can help someone, do; if you can hurt someone, don't.

For years the bumper sticker on my office cubicle offered this message: *And what difference do you make?*

I posted it one day to give myself a boost after hearing too many newspaper readers complain about a column advocating for the poor and powerless.

That bumper sticker became a reminder for me to stay focused on my true calling, to make the difference that Regina Brett is supposed to make. A job isn't just to make a living or a life. It's to make a difference. What imprint will you leave at the end of the day? Is that the imprint you want to leave on coworkers, clients, customers?

Someone once told me, "One day you will be just a memory to people. Do what you can now to make sure it's a good one."

I don't always know if it's a good one. When I was a newspaper reporter, I was often assigned to call people for comments on breaking news. Once, I called a workplace to gather information about a man who had been killed in an accident. The person I spoke to had not yet heard that her friend was killed. I felt awful that she hadn't heard in a more graceful, gentle way from someone who knew her.

Another time, we were all covering the aftermath of the riots at a prison in Lucasville, Ohio. The National Guard had been called in to break up a riot at the Southern Ohio Correctional Facility that killed seven. An editor wanted me to call the victim of one of the inmates who had died in the riot. He had been convicted of kidnapping and raping her at knifepoint ten years earlier.

I dreaded making that call. Wouldn't it just stir up more pain? I prayed before dialing her number. When I asked for her reaction to his death, she screamed. She didn't know he had been killed in the riot.

She started to laugh and cry. Ever since he had attacked her, she'd been afraid of the day he would be free. "I wake up screaming and have headaches. I have nightmares every day," she told me. She was relieved he was gone. "What a blessing."

She thanked me for telling her and for changing her life. She hadn't paid any attention to the news of the riot and no one in her immediate life knew about that rape that had happened ten years ago.

Sometimes it isn't clear if you're doing good or harm. I once wrote a column praising a child for calling the police when she found her mother's drugs. Maybe that mom could get help and not end up like another mom, a drug addict who was murdered and left behind two sons. Unfortunately, I named those kids. Their names had already been used in the newspaper, but I didn't need to use them again.

I saved two of the angry letters I got. One was from a fifth-grade teacher of one of those boys: "Your article not only rehashed the gruesome details of his mother's death (details that the child wasn't aware of) but made the assumption that the boys knew what their mother was doing and should have turned her in...I ask you to please use better judgment when dealing with the feelings of children in the future."

The principal also wrote me. He agreed with the argument I made, but wrote, "You have assisted in victimizing these children...Listing the boys' names has undone what months of work by counselors, teachers, family members and friends have tried to heal."

They taught me a great lesson with that column: If you can help someone, do; if you can hurt someone, don't.

I once wrote a lighthearted column about a dilapidated house my daughter lived in on a college campus with eight guys and one woman. The refrigerator had such a horrible odor, I joked that its previous owner might have been Jeffrey Dahmer. I got a call from an angry reader who reminded me that Dahmer's first victim was from the Akron area. I wrote an apology in my next column.

Now when I'm done with a column, I send it through my "spiritual scanner." I pray over it. I say the Saint Francis prayer and ask that God's grace keep me from hurting anyone.

When one of my columns helps people, they carry it in their wallets, post it on the refrigerator, tuck it into Bibles, mail it to their aunts and uncles, quote it in sermons, and reprint it in newsletters and blogs.

One factory worker called at 3 a.m. after he read a column I wrote about my dad's blue-collar work ethic. The man said he knew he couldn't leave his kids much in terms of money, but when he saw his own values reflected in my column, he knew that's what he was passing on. "I loved that column you wrote about your dad," he said. "I taped it to the inside of my tool-box to remind me why I do what I do."

One woman sent a card that read "If I were a writer, I'd like to know what people thought of my work. Someone on stage can hear the applause; you should know there is a 70-year-old grandma in Wooster clapping for you."

One father invited me to come into his home just hours after his son was gunned down. He trusted me, a stranger, to tell the world what a good son he had lost. I'll never forget how this big electric company lineman broke down weeping as he opened up his worn wallet to hand me the photo of his son.

One woman in blue jeans thanked me for blasting a police chief who had been accused of beating his wife. I didn't know she was an off-duty police officer until she whipped out her badge and told me the officers on her shift appreciated the columns, too.

One woman called to say she found my column of life lessons in her husband's pocket after he died. He lived just 45 days after being diagnosed with cancer.

In every walk of life, there are people who do their best not to hurt others, and people who don't care. I met a public defender who called his clients "dirtballs" and others who worked overtime for free to keep defendants out of prison. I've met police officers who love to hand out tickets to boost their quota and I've met officers who won't ticket cars with expired plates in poor neighborhoods because they know that $100 ticket covers food for a month.

I've met judges who took pleasure in shaming people by giving them absurd sentences to carry out publicly just to get on TV. I've also met judges like Joan Synenberg who were tough yet thoughtful. One defendant wept in her courtroom during sentencing because he had no family and no one to write to him in prison. She promised to write to him and did every month.

It's not about how much power you have at work, but how you choose to use your power. I'll never forget the e-mail I got from a woman named Barb who shared this story with me: She had challenged her granddaughter, Calista, who was eight, to learn how to spell "supercalifragilisticexpialidocious." Within two days, the little girl called and spelled it for her. Barb decided to take her to dinner to celebrate at Macaroni Grill.

She called the restaurant before they arrived and asked if the server could come to their table and ask, "Are you girls celebrating something special tonight?" The person could have said, No, we don't have time for that. Instead, a man named Jim agreed to after he heard about Calista's achievement. When they arrived at the restaurant, he came to their table and asked if they were celebrating anything special.

When Calista told him about her spelling achievement, Jim asked if she knew what movie the word came from. Calista said, "Yes, *Mary Poppins*."

"Do you have the movie?" he asked. She didn't. They had rented it from the library.

"Well, you have the movie now," Jim said, and handed Calista the DVD with a pink bow on top.

Before they left, Calista asked her grandma how the man knew what they were celebrating. The little girl thought he might be a spy, then she decided he was an angel.

He was.

Bottom line?

Be one of the helpers. My daughter grew up watching Mister Rogers. She was glued to the TV every day watching that boring man in the boring cardigan sweater talk slower than molasses. One day I listened. The man spoke like a minister. I didn't know until he died in 2003 that he was an ordained Presbyterian minister.

I never realized the power of his message until we lost 20 children in the shooting at Sandy Hook Elementary School in Newtown, Connecticut. What should we tell our children? How could they ever trust life again? How could we?

People everywhere started quoting, of all people, Mister Rogers. He once shared that when he was a boy and saw scary things in the news, his mom would tell him, "Look for the helpers. You will always find people who are helping." His words helped us all remember that the world is full of helpers.

That's where you find your comfort. You turn your attention away from the hurters and look for the helpers.

Better yet, be one.

It's important to know both your superpower and your kryptonite.

One person can change the world.

How do I know?

I work with Clark Kent.

Seriously.

Michael Sangiacomo is an energetic, curly-haired guy who has the wonder and joy of a ten-year-old boy. Mike is a mild-mannered reporter at the *Plain Dealer* who refuses to grow up. He still reads comics. He writes comics. He still believes in superheroes. Still believes Superman can fly.

Good thing.

A while back, Mike took on something brave and bold and slightly crazy. He believed he could save Superman's house. The real thing. The real, live, bricks-and-mortar three-story blue house with the red trim at 10622 Kimberly Avenue.

The Man of Steel was born in Cleveland, Ohio, more than 75 years ago.

The house nearly died of neglect despite its occupants' efforts to maintain it. Then one day a writer came to town. Novelist Brad Meltzer wanted to see the very room where two kids in the Glenville neighborhood created the biggest superhero known to man. The owners granted Brad a tour. Brad shared that tour in a video he made to help save Superman's home at www.OrdinaryPeopleChangeTheWorld.com. There he told viewers, "I believe ordinary people change the world."

Ordinary people? Not superheroes?

"Want to know how the world got Superman?" Brad said. "Because two kids, Jerry Siegel and Joe Shuster, who were so poor that they used to draw on the back of wallpaper, came up with the idea for a bulletproof man that they named Superman."

In the video, he walks into Superman's house and shows us room by room how Cleveland, Ohio, failed to preserve the famous house decades ago. The walls and ceiling rotted away. Red tape holds up a light switch. It's sad as the music on the video plays the song lyric "Even heroes have the right to dream."

He made me think of those nights I spent as a child imagining a bigger, better me while reading those comics under the covers.

"People think that Superman is the important part," Brad said. "The best part of the story? Clark Kent."

The mild-mannered reporter?

"Wanna know why?" Brad asked. "'Cause we're Clark Kent. I love the idea that all of us, in all our ordinariness, want to do something better, want to be something better, that we can tear open our shirt and try and help people."

We all have a superpower. We all possess some ability that defines us. We also have our own kryptonite, something that confines us, something that robs us of our strengths, drains us of our powers, weakens us in an instant. Usually our greatest strengths and our greatest weaknesses are cousins.

For Superman, it was kryptonite. A slice of his home planet, Krypton, made him crumble. He could leap tall buildings in a single bound, race a locomotive and win, and spin the world back to yesterday, but expose him to a bit of kryptonite, and he couldn't walk around the block.

My greatest power is speaking up for others. My kryptonite is not ever feeling worthy enough to speak up. All through my childhood, I couldn't speak up to my dad to stop him from hitting my brothers and sisters. I couldn't speak up to the kids at school who made fun of me for being skinny, for having hairy arms and big ears and glasses. I couldn't speak up to the kids who teased and tormented a girl in eighth grade because she didn't know to use deodorant. I couldn't speak up for the boy who got shoved into lockers and pushed around in high school because he was gay.

As a columnist, I've used my voice to speak out against child abuse, bullying, and all sorts of social injustice. I've taken on judges, prosecutors, and governors. Still, some days it's hard to find my voice when I need to return a sweater and don't have the receipt.

My friend Beth found her superpower in helping babies in medical distress. She has spent her entire career as a child life specialist at Rainbow Babies & Children's Hospital in Cleveland, advocating for children before, during, and after medical tests and procedures. Her kryptonite? Deep down, under all that joy helping parents and children feel safer at the hospital, is a terrible sense of powerlessness over losing her own newborn son whom she never brought home from the hospital. Beth had diabetes, which weakened her body so much she couldn't carry her baby to full term. Her son was born too early. The loss of the only child she ever gave birth to is where Beth gets both her superpower and her kryptonite.

A good friend of mine is a perfectionist. That is both his superpower and his kryptonite. He suffers from obsessive-compulsive disorder. When we go on vacation together, he brings cleaning supplies to spray down the bedroom and the bathroom. The plus side? Here's what he does for a living: he's paid to find errors in commercial leases.

My husband runs a crisis communications firm. He absolutely loves to help people get through their worst moments. A chemical company had a spill one night and called at 2 a.m. Bruce stayed on the phone for hours and calmly walked them through who to call and what to say to the employees, media, and residents who had to be evacuated. He's great in a crisis, but is constantly weakened by his own worst moment, by the one crisis in his life that he couldn't stop.

He got the call that his mom died when he was 22. She had been talking on the phone to a friend when she suddenly dropped dead. Barbara was just 45. The coroner called it atypical pneumonia. No one knew she was sick. It was a crisis that rocked the family. He had a brother who had recently graduated from college and a brother and sister still in middle school when she died. The family had just sold their home and was planning to move the week she died. Not a day goes by that he doesn't miss her; not a week goes by that he doesn't wish he could have done more to help his siblings through that awful time.

His brother Gary never got over losing his mom and his home all in the same week. He owns and operates Gary Hennes Realtors and specializes in finding people the homes of their dreams in South Beach. He wants them to find their sense of place in the world, something he still struggles to find for himself. His superpower is to bring beauty into every building and condo he encounters and help create a home for the right owner. His kryptonite? A lovely woman named Barbara who tugs at his heart so hard, it's difficult to let anyone else into it.

We all have a superpower, even the most ordinary among us.

That's how the video on saving Superman's house ends. The people trying to save Superman's house are just ordinary Clark Kent types.

"You know who's going to save it?" Brad asks. "We are. Regular ordinary people."

People like him. People like Mike. People like us. The video ends with a string of ordinary people proclaiming, "I am Superman."

We all are.

Inside of me, inside of you, inside of us, we all have the power. The power to change the world, or at least our small corner of it.

God completes our work.

The emergency call came while I was inside the ambulance restocking bandages on the shelves above the cot: *possible heart attack*.

The victim was in Atwater, a farming community 15 minutes away. We flew at 80 miles an hour with lights and sirens, zipping past cornfields and barns, past women hanging out clothes and children chasing collies. The training I received as an emergency medical technician flooded my head as the adrenaline flowed through my body. Clear the airway, check the vital signs, check for history of heart disease, et cetera. When we got to the scene I was ready for this man and his heart.

What I wasn't ready for was a little boy.

People flagged us down at the scene and led us to a backyard where a small crowd clustered around a body. I pushed my way through them and someone pulled the blanket off. I expected an old man. The first thing I saw was a sneaker smaller than my hand. The boy was about seven years old, had blond hair, and was wearing blue jeans. He wasn't breathing. I lifted his small head and put my fingers on his neck; no pulse. I tipped his head back, pinched his nose, and blew into his mouth. His chest rose like a balloon. Another ambulance attendant started CPR and counted out loud, "One thousand one, one thousand two..."

I scanned the backyard. There was a rope at the foot of a nearby tree. No one there knew who the boy was or what happened. My heart was silently screaming, *Where are his parents? What is his name? Who is this little boy?* I wanted to stroke his blond hair and hold him, talk to him, love him into life, but I had no free hand for comfort, no free breath for words. When I tilted his head back, I saw a half-inch-wide red ring across the front of his neck. It stretched from ear to ear. I checked his pupils and looked into the bluest eyes I had ever seen. They were quickly dissolving into black. His skin was still warm, and so, so soft.

With every breath, I breathed in a prayer: *God, don't let this little boy die. Please, let him live.* If only I could will him to life, pray him to life, breathe him to life.

The ride to the hospital seemed like both an eternity and a mere second in time. At the hospital, three doctors and five nurses met us at the emergency room door. They hovered over the boy as I stood in the hall, praying for a miracle. I couldn't even pray for him by name. We had no idea who he was or what had happened. The doctors zapped his heart, pumped oxygen into him, rubbed his limbs for over an hour, but the red ring on his neck never faded. It was as if death left a permanent smile, mocking us all. My ambulance crew didn't leave until we saw the white sheet of surrender cover him.

I thought of his parents coming home or getting the call. The world would end for them. It wouldn't matter what they owned, what jobs they held, what their income was. Their son was dead. In the bathroom outside the ER, I punched the wall with one hand and wiped away tears with the other. The next day I read in the newspaper that the child had been accidentally strangled on a rope while playing in a tree.

Every October, I think about that boy. The breath that left his lips had smelled like tomatoes ripening in the sun. Every autumn, when that scent brings him back, I blow him a kiss, wherever he is, and pray for his parents.

There are times in your life when you do the best you can and your best isn't enough. You don't get the happy ending. You don't get the job you wanted or the raise you deserved or the promotion you earned. You don't get the high fives and pats on the back and fist bumps. You go home broken and sad and exhausted and wonder what the hell happened. And you don't get an answer. You just have to go back to work and do your best again and again, without fail, no matter how you think you failed. God completes our work, makes it complete in ways that sometimes remain a mystery to us, a mystery that isn't ours to solve, but ours to accept.

In my career as a journalist, it has often been my job to interview people about their worst day. I'm not talking about the bad day at work because the copier broke or the boss yelled at you or the vending machine ate your dollar. I'm talking about when the patient dies or the plane doesn't land the way it's supposed to or the bad guy can't be stopped in time.

I've never forgotten a flight attendant who shared her story of survival with me. She showed me the uniform she wore the day that United Airlines Flight 232 crashed in a cornfield in Sioux City in 1989. I spoke to her six months after the crash, the week she was to return to work. She held up the uniform she had worn the day of the crash. She wouldn't wash the dirty white blouse with the gold-and-navy epaulets. The blood on it wasn't hers. It was the imprint left when a wounded passenger hugged her.

Susan talked about the faces of those who died. They weren't strangers; they were the women she had chatted with on the plane, the men she had comforted with pillows, the children she had poured sodas for and smiled at. She remembered all those people whose tears she couldn't stop, who kept crying, "Are we going to die?" Susan kept telling them, "I don't know. Keep praying." There's no way to understand why 112 people died that day and why she lived.

Then there was the police chief in Brimfield, Ohio, who told me about his worst day at work. "January 21, 2005," David Oliver said. "It wasn't just the worst day of work. It was the worst day of my life."

A woman in his small town of 10,000 people had tried to flee her abusive boyfriend. Renee Bauer had her coat on, a bag packed, and was ready to escape with her son, Dakota, who was seven. James Trimble stopped her with his gun. She tried to shield her son, but the bullets went through her and killed him, too. Renee and Dakota are buried in the cemetery behind the Brimfield Police Department. The chief goes to the gravesite every week.

"It makes me feel I'm taking care of them now," he said.

The man who killed them fled the scene before police arrived and took a Kent State University student hostage. Chief Oliver remembers trying to negotiate for her freedom. He can still hear the woman slowly spelling her last name for him over the phone. Sarah Positano was shot and died before the police could reach her. Trimble was arrested, tried, and sentenced to death.

The chief told me he still loves his job, but to love it, you have to make peace with the things you can't change and summon the courage to change the things you can. You simply keep doing your best to make a difference wherever you can. He works hard to catch the bad guys, but he also goes to the elementary school every morning to high-five every child who walks in the door. He organizes events like Shop with a Cop, where a hundred children each get $100 to buy anything they want. Or Fill-a-Cruiser, where police park cruisers at area stores and people fill them with toys and food for the local food cupboard. He has breakfast with hundreds of senior citizens so shut-ins don't feel so alone.

Your worst day at work might scar you for life, but it doesn't have to scare you away from the work you love. If you let that scar make you stronger, then, in time, it will make the world around you stronger, too.

Not everything that counts can be counted.

Most of us won't end up famous, but wouldn't it be great to be unforgettable?

Or to leave a mark behind that is?

Those people are called teachers.

Andy Rooney used to say that most people don't end up with more than a handful of people who remember them, but teachers have thousands who will remember them for the rest of their lives.

I once wrote a column encouraging readers to write a six-word memoir. These entries were penned by teachers:

Making a difference. Leaving a legacy.

Shaping the future in the present.

Teachers wanted: Patience mandatory, sanity optional.

Hoped to make difference. Was transformed.

I just want to teach. Period.

The last one could be echoed by teachers everywhere.

Unfortunately, tests have taken over teaching. The way we measure the worth of a teacher is no longer by the impact or imprint they leave on a student's life, but by the grade the student leaves on a test score. Too often the worth of a student is reduced to a number on a state proficiency test, graduation test, GPA, SAT, or ACT.

I love the apology that Principal David Root wrote to parents of students at Rocky River Middle School in Ohio after the report cards came out one June.

The children did well on the 2008 Ohio Achievement Tests that were required to be given each year to assess math, reading, science, social studies, and writing skills among all the state's public school students in grades three through eight. The school earned an "Excellent" rating and met the mandates for Adequate Yearly Progress. But what was the cost to the students and staff to focus so much on testing all year long? Where did they lose their focus? In far too many classrooms, teachers spent most of their time teaching children how to pass the state's proficiency tests. He lamented what wasn't getting taught, those experiences and the knowledge that can't be measured or counted in numbers.

For all those accomplishments, the principal had only one thing to say to the students, staff, and citizens of Rocky River: I'm sorry.

Mr. Root issued an apology. He sent it to me typed out in two pages, single-spaced. His apology made me think about how we can lose focus on what really matters when we insist on using measuring sticks to evaluate success.

He was sorry that his teachers spent less time teaching

American history because most of the social studies test questions were about foreign countries.

Sorry that he didn't suspend a student for assaulting another because the attacker would have missed valuable test days.

He was sorry for pulling children away from art, music, and gym, classes they loved, so they could learn test-taking strategies.

Sorry that he had to give a test for which he couldn't clarify any questions, make any comments to help in understanding, or share the results so students could actually learn from their mistakes.

Sorry that he kept students in school after they became sick during the test, because if they couldn't finish the test as a result of illness, the students would automatically fail it.

Sorry that the integrity of his teachers was publicly tied to one test.

He apologized for losing eight days of instruction because of testing activities.

For making decisions on assemblies, field trips, and musical performances based on how that time away from reading, math, social studies, and writing would affect state test results.

For arranging for some students to be labeled "at risk" in front of their peers and put in small groups so the school would have a better chance of passing tests.

For no longer focusing as a principal on helping his staff teach students but rather on helping them teach test indicators.

Mr. Root isn't anti-tests. He's all for tests that measure progress and help set teaching goals. But in his eyes, state achievement tests were designed for the media to show how schools rank against one another.

When I spoke to him, he had been a principal for 24 years, half of them at Rocky River Middle School, the rest in the cities of Hudson, Alliance, and Zanesville, Ohio. He loves working with sixth, seventh, and eighth graders. "I have a strong compassion for the puberty-stricken," he joked.

His students, who are ages 11, 12, 13, and 14, worry that teachers they love will be let go based on how well they perform. One asked him, "If I don't do well, will you fire my teacher?" He cringed when he heard one say, "I really want to do well, but I'm not that smart."

He wants students to learn how to think, not how to take tests.

"We don't teach kids anymore," he said. "We teach test-taking skills. We all teach to the test. I long for the days when we used to teach kids."

The way we judge teachers makes me think of that beautiful quote attributed to Albert Einstein: "Not everything that counts can be counted and not everything that can be counted counts."

That's so true about teachers. But it's true about the rest of us as well.

Too often employers create ways to count, quantify, or measure our worth, yet those methods barely come close to valuing what really matters. We're measured by performance reviews, evaluations, critiques, the number of widgets produced, sales figures, customers served, or clicks on a website. I remember an editor who used to do a byline count to see how many stories a year every writer produced. It made reporters cringe. Was it really all about numbers? Accountability is important, but you can't quantify everything.

It's not always the boss who tries to quantify our worth. Sometimes we do it to ourselves. We constantly find ways to measure our worth outside of ourselves and we never measure up. We obsessively check the number of friends and followers we have on Facebook and Twitter. I used to count the number of calls and e-mails I got on a column to see how much it mattered. The truth is there is no way to measure the love that goes into the work that we do or the worth that others see in us.

Not everything that counts can be counted. Early in my journalism career, an editor passed along a story that I've never forgotten. It's been handed down to countless journalists. A reporter named Al Martinez was working late one Christmas Eve for the *Oakland Tribune*. He was writing about a boy who was dying of leukemia. The boy's greatest wish? Fresh peaches.

Such a simple, small wish.

It was a perfect tearjerker story for readers to wake up to on Christmas. The reporter was typing away on the story when the phone rang around 11 p.m. The city editor asked what he was working on. The reporter told him about the dying boy and the peaches and how there weren't any fresh peaches, but it was a good story. There was space reserved on the front page for it, the prime real estate every reporter shoots for every time, the true measure of greatness achieved in a newsroom.

The editor asked how long the boy had to live. The reporter said, Not long. Days. After a long pause, the editor told him, "Get the kid his peaches."

The reporter had tried. He had already called all over. Peaches were out of season. The editor persisted. Call all over the globe if you have to. Do whatever it takes.

The reporter made hasty calls as his deadline neared and finally, magically it seemed, he found peaches and arranged a plane to fly them in so the boy could receive them. There was barely time to write the story. Deadline was looming large when the editor called again and asked him to deliver the peaches to the boy. The reporter said time was running out; he had to start writing the story to get it in the paper.

The editor told him, "I didn't say get the story. I said get the kid his peaches."

The boy got his peaches. The readers got the story. The reporter got his byline. And the rest of us got the message: what counts most isn't our work, but the humanity that goes into it.

Don't confuse your work with your worth.

It's strange how Father's Day sneaks up on you after you've lost your dad.

You forget the day is coming, then, *bam!*, it's there. You pass the greeting card section in the store, stop and pull out a card, then realize there's nobody to send it to.

My dad has been gone for 16 years, but I can still hear his voice and feel remnants of him everywhere. I've never forgotten the winter night I borrowed his car and was driving home late. Snow was coming down so hard you could hardly see the road. I was just a block from home when I saw a ghostly figure walking in the middle of the road. What nut was out walking on a night like tonight?

My dad.

He was carrying a space heater to a family a few blocks away. They had no heat. They called him to fix their furnace but he couldn't get it working, so he took them one of our space heaters.

That's the kind of dad he was.

His sister Kate once told us that our dad never had a childhood. He always worked, even as a child. He was the oldest son, which meant the burden always fell on him. He got yelled at for feeding the horses extra grain when they were dying of starvation during the Depression. It must have broken his heart to see them wither away.

My aunts told me about the day they lost the farm. They were in the house and listened as the auctioneer sold everything they owned and loved, from the house to the horses to the corn in the fields. My dad, Tom Brett, had planted that corn. He was just 20 years old. The auctioneer said the $690 for the crop would go to my dad.

He used the money for a down payment on a shack by the railroad tracks on Sycamore Street in Ravenna, Ohio. It was the only place the family could afford. The neighbors couldn't believe anyone would move into it. My dad and his brothers scared out all the critters and then dug out a basement. The second floor had one bedroom. They turned it into three.

As time went on, my dad and mom lived in that house. Dad kept adding more rooms as he added kids.

My dad never worried about furthering his education. He quit school after eighth grade to support his family. He spent his life in blue-collared shirts with a red bandanna in his back pocket to wipe off his sweat. The only time he left his small town was to fight a big war. He was a tail gunner in World War II and flew more than 30 missions. He cried every time one of us left for big cities like New York, D.C., Phoenix, Chicago, and even Cleveland. If he'd had it his way, we'd all still be living in Ravenna.

Dad was a workaholic. He had no hobbies. He never stopped working. He expected us to do the same.

When our punishment wasn't the belt, it was work. Sweep the floors. Mop the dining room. Sort nails in the Shop. He always called his garage the Shop. It was the original Home Depot. Somehow he knew where every screw and bolt and nail belonged. So did my five brothers. Anytime they committed a misdemeanor, like breaking a lamp while wrestling in the living room, Dad would bark, "I've got some nails for you to sort," and lead them to a workbench with a giant pickle jar full of every size of nail known to wood.

If we were playing, he'd yell, "Go help your mother." If we were reading, he'd say, "You'll never learn anything from those." We dreaded these words: "I've got a job for you."

Work defined him. When he lost his job, it shattered him. I still don't know what happened. He had me type page after page of angry rants to the union, the company, whoever it was that took away his livelihood. He never got it back. I watched my six-foot-two dad shrink before my eyes. He was lost. My mom got a part-time job working nights at traffic court to help pay the bills.

It killed my dad. His wife was working and he wasn't.

When she took on more hours to help clean the church, he got angry. He accused her of spending too much time there. He was bitter. His reaction was almost like she was having an affair. With who, God?

Finally, he went into business for himself and the world righted itself. He recruited my brothers to help with roofing jobs, ductwork, and fixing furnaces. Somehow he always outworked them.

My dad never took a vacation. Ever. When we got spring break, we didn't get a vacation either. Ever. There were no trips to the beach or Disneyland. Ever. We spent our week off cleaning out the freezer in the basement, scrubbing the dining room chairs, all 13 of them, or washing down the wood paneling in the living room.

Did he like his work? We never knew. You never asked that kind of question back then. He liked not being poor. He liked not being hungry. He liked making our lives better than his ever was.

When he had a heart attack in his 70s, he took the wooden ladders off the roof of the station wagon before driving himself to the hospital so my mom wouldn't have to drive home from the hospital with them on the roof.

As much as I admired his work ethic, it was both a blessing and a curse. It still is. Sometimes your parents teach you lessons that you have to unlearn. It took a long time for me to realize my work wasn't my worth.

I still find it hard to relax. I still feel guilty taking a vacation. I still struggle with calling out of work when I'm sick. If I do call in sick, I usually end up doing the laundry, dusting the furniture, or cleaning out a drawer just to feel useful. Even the year I had breast cancer, when I had two surgeries, four months of chemotherapy, and six weeks of daily radiation, I missed just two weeks of work. I scheduled my chemo around my job, so I would be sick on the weekend and able to recover for work on Monday. I sobbed when I finally had to call out from sheer exhaustion. Who was I if I wasn't working?

Who was I? A child of God who was already worthy enough. I remember how I balked when a priest told me God didn't care a whit about all my doing. "God delights in your presence," he said.

But I could give God so much more than that, I thought.

"Your presence matters more than your performance," the priest kept telling me.

That's what mattered most about our dad. His presence, not his work.

When he was present pulling us on the metal saucer sled through the snow, or taking a break from work to run the bases with us in a game of kickball, or taking us fishing with those bamboo poles and bobbers, and all those times he came home from work happy and yelled as he opened the door, "I'm home, you lucky people!"

Yes, we were lucky.

I thought of that as I walked through the Shop one day and caught a whiff of the sawdust from the lumber he helped us turn into birdhouses and caught sight of those fishing poles and that old beat-up sled. I poked around his workbench and found a big grocery bag. I couldn't believe what was inside.

Every Father's Day card we ever sent him.

I used to worry that as time wore out the roofs and furnaces he installed, my dad's work would be gone. Whenever we went for a drive, he used to point out every roof, as if it was a work of art he had created. But his work wasn't his legacy.

Blue-collar guys like my dad didn't worry about leaving a mark on the world. They never focused on climbing a career ladder to reach some lofty goal or holy grail. They were too busy climbing real ladders to keep roofs over their families' heads. My dad held the ladder for us to climb higher than he ever got to.

We were his grail.

He left his mark on us, and because of that, he is in every mark my siblings and I leave on the world.

*Clear the path for the person who comes
after you.*

W hat advice do you wish you had known before starting
your career?

Jessica Thomas answered that question in a handbook she
wrote called "Advice for College to My Little Sister." She typed
it up and gave it to her younger sister as a high school graduation gift.

Jessica was 23 and a graduate student in biomedical engi-
neering at Ohio State University when she decided to clear the
path for her sister. Rachel was 18 and an incoming freshman at
Ohio Wesleyan. They're both from North Olmsted, Ohio. Jessica took everything she learned in four years and condensed
it into five pages.

"The most difficult moment is when your parents leave,"
Jessica wrote. "But remember, it's like when you were 2 and
were left with a babysitter for the first time—you freak out for

about 10 minutes, then you're fine." When your parents drive away, you panic for a few minutes in fear: "Oh, no, I'm on my own." Then the excitement kicks in, and it becomes "Oh, wow, I'm on my own!"

The first year you can feel lost and confused. The second year, you own the place. You catch yourself telling your parents, "I'm going home," and by "home," you mean your dorm.

As the protective older sib, Jessica wanted to make the transition easier for her sister. It was all the stuff she wished she would have known. Reading Jessica's handbook made me wish I had both received one from my four older sibs and written one for my six younger sibs.

After I got pregnant at 21 and dropped out of college, I worked a series of jobs to pay the rent and ended up as a secretary. I've never forgotten the day my oldest sister, Therese, challenged me to finish college. She did it with one single sentence: "Do you want to be a secretary the rest of your life?"

Now, if you love being a secretary and are great at it, your answer might be a joyful, resounding "Yes!" But I sucked at it and hated the job. Still, I got mad at her for making me feel so small. How dare she insult me. The truth is, no one can make you feel small. What she did was remind me that I felt small because I was settling for something smaller than my own dream.

We weren't taught how to dream. We were taught how to survive. My dad never got to dream. He dropped out of school after eighth grade to support his family after they lost everything in the Depression. He spent his life carrying shingles and spouting up ladders in the hot sun. In the winter, he fixed furnaces full of asbestos, which ended up killing him. He had hoped his five sons would take over the Brett Sheet Metal family business. They didn't want any part of that backbreaking work that paid so little and took so much out of them.

My mom never went to college. She worked as a nurse's aide until she met my dad. He was a handsome bachelor who was a patient in the hospital. She either accidentally or on purpose burned him with a hot water bottle so he had to stay longer. They married, agreed to have 10 kids, and ended up with 11. One was an accident. They never told us which.

It was hard on them when the first child left for college. I think they felt abandoned or betrayed. They wanted us to live at home or at least in our hometown forever. When my sister Patricia got a scholarship to Yale, they spoke about it in hushed tones, whispering, "Why does she have to leave Ohio?" They had no idea what an incredible achievement it was for her.

My siblings forged their own paths. I remember my sister Therese in that unflattering matronly uniform she wore at the Acme grocery store in our hometown as she worked her way through college ringing up groceries. She was the first to attend college, but she commuted from home. She ended up with several careers. Her last one was saving lives as an ICU nurse before she retired.

My sister Joan was the first to move out to live in a dorm at college. My parents wanted us to go to the closest and cheapest university, Kent State University, which was six miles away. Joan was the pioneer who set her sights on Ohio State University, two and a half hours away. It meant moving out and supporting herself. Joan ended up with a PhD in organizational psychology from New York University and is a professor at Arizona State University.

My brother Michael got his MBA at Ohio State and became a CPA. Mary, who worked a factory job at General Electric for years to pay for college, got two master's degrees and has saved countless souls who have suffered from domestic violence and drug and alcohol addictions.

Tom spent years working on roofs with my dad, graduated from Kent State, and does real-estate appraisals and works for the Ohio Department of Transportation.

Maureen went to Bowling Green State University and got a degree in journalism. She ended up marketing homes and services for a retirement community that makes seniors feel at home in the world.

Patricia went to Ohio State, then got her master's degree in architecture at Yale. I love walking past the building she designed in New York City. Then she went on to design her own line of Veronica Brett swimwear that was featured in *O, Oprah's* magazine.

Mark got a degree in physical therapy from Ohio State, earned an MBA, and now oversees several hospitals in Michigan. Jim got an accounting degree from Kent State, joined the Peace Corps, and served in Uzbekistan. He's now a CPA in Washington, D.C.

Matthew, the baby, spent his childhood drawing comics. Being the last of 11 made him bolder. He once told my parents he was going camping and drove to New Jersey to see Bruce Springsteen. Another time he told them he was going fishing and went skydiving. He graduated from Kent State with a degree in graphic design. I never realized how hard it was for him to pave his own way until years after he opened his own graphic design firm in Chicago called Substance.

Back when he was still living at home with Mom and Dad, he got an interview in Chicago. When it ended, they said, "Can you start in two weeks?" He said yes, not having a clue how he would break the news to our folks that he was moving out in two weeks. How would he tell them that after raising 11 children, they would soon be empty nesters? How would he find an apartment? How would he get there? How would he get around? Moving from Ravenna, Ohio (population 12,000), to Chicago (population 2.7 million) can seem like a trip to the moon when you're the first one to do it.

I wish I could have helped him, but back then I was too lost to know how to clear the way for the next traveler. I didn't even know it was my job to do so. Now I do. We all do. Each of my siblings has helped clear the way for the nieces and nephews that came after us.

My husband and I have used the third floor of our old home as a launching pad, first for our own kids, then for our niece Rachel, who left a job in Dayton to come to Cleveland. She ended up getting a job at the Rock and Roll Hall of Fame. She got an apartment, met the love of her life, and lives nearby with her husband and son.

My nephew Michael is pursuing a PhD. He knows it's possible because his aunt has one. His sister Leah played in the marching band in her high school in Garrettsville, Ohio, population 2,329. She ended up in the marching band for Notre Dame, playing in the band on national TV in front of millions. She just got a master's in dance therapy in Boston. Her brother Luke starred in high school theater productions, spent a summer living in our house to work at a theater camp, wrote a play, then spent a summer studying theater at the Stella Adler Studio in New York City. He graduated with a theater degree from Baldwin Wallace University.

I'm still in awe that each of my ten siblings left home and pursued their dreams. That old adage "Reach for the moon; even if you miss you'll land among the stars" describes them all. They are all stars to me, and a light for the next generation of stars.

Just because someone isn't on your path doesn't mean they're lost.

Whand my daughter was 23, she fell into a funk.

Her friend who lived in Manhattan was talking about moving to L.A. Her friend who grew up in Kent was heading for Atlanta. Her friends who were getting married were into couplehood. Her friends who were having babies were into motherhood.

Gabrielle found herself stuck in the quarterlife crisis. It hits sometime in the 20s, when you're trying to get a life but everyone else's life looks better than yours. At first I thought my daughter was alone in this quandary. Then she showed me an anonymous e-mail circulating among her friends. It answered the question: How do you know you've moved into adulthood?

"You keep more food than beer in the fridge. You hear your favorite song on an elevator. You don't know what time Taco

147

Bell closes anymore. You no longer take naps from noon to 6 p.m. You go from 130 days of vacation time to 7."

That last one was killing my daughter. She used to work every summer—on her tan. For the first time in her life, she had a real job, a nine-to-five that didn't allow for tanning between noon and two o'clock. She loved the job; she just hated the concept of working nine to five for the rest of her life. I remember the day the realization of finishing school for good hit her and she said to me, "You mean I'm going to have to work every summer for the rest of my life?"

My daughter graduated from college engaged to a great guy. The plan was to get a career job using that $50,000 communications degree and live at home to save money for a fall wedding. As they say, life is what happens when you're making other plans. Life happened. After four months, she quit the job that required her to work 12-hour days for 8 hours' pay. Then somewhere between booking a reception hall and shopping for a wedding gown, she wasn't ready to get married and gave back the ring.

She got a new job, but she wasn't sure what would happen next. She looked for an apartment but couldn't afford much. She struggled to build a life that no longer came with a blueprint. Basically, she was adrift.

I tried to be her anchor, but that didn't help her move on. It was great having her around the house to watch reruns of *Friends*, try new recipes, and take long walks together. Then one week she scared me by checking out flights to Atlanta and New York City. Worried that she might be tempted to move, I suggested she might want to get an apartment here first.

"I don't want to be stuck in this town forever," she sighed.

Stuck in this town? This is Cleveland, I reminded her, land of opportunities, home of the Rock Hall, the Flats, the Tribe, not some Podunk small town with nothing to do. She rolled her eyes. Anywhere your parents live is a town too small.

Living at home too long can make an adult child regress. Parents, too. Hover too long, and you hurt the child's social life and motivation to move on. I thought I was giving her a financial cushion to help her. It turned out that cushion was suffocating her. I wanted to tell her it was okay to fail, to take a risk, to choose something—a city, a career, a guy, a hobby—and build a life. It won't be perfect. No life is.

Life is messy. The five-year plan is highly overrated. Most of the things I planned in life never took. Most of the things that took, I never planned. So far, it's turned out to be a life better than anything I could have imagined. One day she would re- alize that the world is her oyster. But back then, my pearls of wisdom were useless. It was time for her to discover her own, and she did, without me writing out a map for her. She forged her own path by listening to her own heart, not mine.

Sometimes you have to get lost to find yourself. My nephew Michael did just that after he graduated college. He had a plan: three guys, a van, and a map. It didn't sound like much of a plan to me, but Michael counted on it to carry him all the way from Ohio to the University of New Mexico. He was setting out for graduate school. The 26-hour drive from rural Garrettsville, Ohio, to Albuquerque would take a mere three days, he said.

I've seen too many independent films to think it was a good idea. A lot can happen between here and New Mexico to a guy with Ohio plates, long hair, and three guitars. I wanted to save him from breaking down, going broke, or getting lost. So

I made him an offer. As a graduation gift, I would fly him to New Mexico. I was giddy when I presented the offer.

He turned me down flat. He and his buddies wanted to take a road trip in his friend's van.

How many miles were on it?

He didn't know.

Was he covered under the insurance?

He didn't know.

What kind of shape was the van in?

He didn't know.

I kept picturing him lost in the middle of nowhere.

But I couldn't stop him.

Then I left for my own road trip to the beach. My husband wanted to make sure we didn't get lost the way we did the previous year while I was driving, so he bought a GPS. How could I argue? I'm the one who missed the exit and drove a half hour before realizing it.

The GPS looked like a tiny TV stuck to the windshield. The map unfolded on screen as you drove. If you took a wrong turn, it told you to take a U-turn. A female voice told you where to go. "In 800 yards, turn left onto the motorway," she said. After about 20 minutes, I wanted to tell her where to go. I don't like someone telling me how to drive every five minutes, especially some stranger with a British accent who called every interstate "the motorway."

"Isn't this great?" my husband chirped.

No. I hated it. He snored away in the passenger seat, trusting our ride to an anonymous compass.

It's not so bad getting lost, I pouted. It merely extends the vacation. One year we ended up lost but found a lovely view of the Shenandoah Valley. One year we found ourselves on a tiny road no wider than a hair on the map. We saw a sign with a large *L*. Lost? No. It signaled the old Lincoln Highway. My husband perked up. His great uncle, Mike Singer, hiked from New Jersey to San Francisco on it in 1914. His uncle was 18. What a wild trip that must have been. The massive mountain in front of us didn't look so daunting when we pictured him climbing it.

Unfortunately, the next year, our GPS kept us on track and on time. My husband was happy, but I felt robbed by the perfection of it all. There's so much of America to explore. With MapQuest, Google, or a GPS, the art of getting lost is becoming a lost art. I miss the old days when you trusted a map and the man at Texaco to be your guide. Or you just hopped in the car and followed your inner compass.

I thought about that when I said good-bye to Michael. By then, his plans had changed. Three guys and a van turned into two guys and a car. The guy with the van had backed out. But instead of giving him advice, I gave Michael my atlas full of states I've only dreamed of seeing. I was no longer worried that he would get lost.

Truth is, I envied him. He squeezed everything he owned in the back of a Dodge Neon and no one was telling him where to go on the motorway.

He did end up getting lost an hour from home before he even left Ohio. Then the power steering and air-conditioning broke and they melted all the way to Albuquerque.

He got lost, but he found himself on the journey. He is finishing a master's degree in philosophy and is ready to tackle his PhD. He's not sure where that will happen, but he'll forge his own path and do it his way.

Expand your comfort zone to make others more comfortable.

Minutes before I walked onstage to give a keynote address at a business conference, a woman approached me to ask a question.

She was the interpreter for the event at a local university and asked if it was all right if she signed my speech for anyone in the audience who was hearing-impaired or deaf. She didn't want to be a distraction but wanted to share my message.

Of course it was fine, I told her. I warned her that I talked fast and might be hard to follow. She laughed.

We had a few minutes, so I asked what got her interested in sign language. I thought she might have been raised by a deaf parent or had someone hard of hearing in her immediate family.

She told me a lovely story I've never forgotten.

She was just 14 that summer she worked at the ice cream shop. One day a man walked in and held up a sign: *one large chocolate cone*. She thought he was a bit odd, but she scooped the cone and handed it to him. Whenever he came in, he always held up the sign for the same order: *one large chocolate cone*. It finally hit the young girl that the man was deaf.

So she got a book out of the library and taught herself some sign language. It took her half an hour to learn one question for her customer. The next time the man came into the ice cream parlor, she signed the words: *How may I help you?*

He was stunned.

So stunned he left the store without even getting his large chocolate cone. Did she sign the wrong words? Did she somehow offend him?

Minutes later he came back. He brought with him a carload of deaf friends.

They came into the ice cream shop, he looked at her then signed to them, they looked at her, and they all started to cry. I cried when I found out the woman became a professional interpreter and a college professor who teaches sign language for a living.

Incredible things can happen for us and others when we expand our comfort zones to make someone else comfortable. Instead of searching for our career paths, sometimes the paths find us outside of our comfort zones.

Annette Fisher was comfortable running a bridal store until she volunteered to take care of a friend's farm animals while the woman was on vacation. While Annette was feeding the animals, she noticed a dark corner of the barn stall full of cobwebs. She brushed them away and discovered a crippled pig. The potbellied pig had been neglected and looked as if its legs had been broken. The pig had no hair and couldn't walk. It turned out the pig had once been fat and happy until someone dropped her while unloading her from a truck.

Annette's career path had taken her into graphic design. She owned an advertising agency for 11 years, got married, bought a few acres, and owned the bridal shop. She had reached all her goals at age 26, but something was missing. Her "aha moment" came the day she took that sick pig to work to give it medicine. A bride-to-be was upset that the Alfred Angelo gown she was trying on didn't match her shoes and purse. As Annette watched the woman in the designer dress, she looked at the pig and realized she'd rather be working with the pig.

"When you look at the big picture, no one really cares if your shoes match your dress," Annette told me.

When the farm owner returned and asked how much money she owed Annette for taking care of the animals, Annette told her, "How about you just give me that crippled pig?"

That pig haunted her. Annette wondered how many other farms had animals like that, abused, neglected, or forgotten in dark musty stalls. Annette closed the bridal shop and opened Happy Trails Farm Animal Sanctuary.

Annette pampered the pig until Janice died seven years later in 2007. She calls Janice the founder of Happy Trails. Annette fed the pig peppermints, and Janice lived out her last days in a tiny log cabin with heat lamps. She slept under a thick pink comforter beneath a piggy pinup calendar on the wall.

Annette has since expanded Happy Trails Farm Animal

Sanctuary in Ravenna, Ohio, the town where I grew up. Once word got out about her refuge, the Humane Society, Animal Protective League, and law enforcement officers started bringing in abused and neglected animals. She has barns full of hogs, horses, ducks, geese, and chickens. Happy Trails has rescued more than 4,000 animals. The nonprofit finds foster and adoptive homes for farm animals. Volunteers clean stalls, repair fences, build shelters, and unload hay. The farm's mission is to rescue, rehabilitate, and adopt out animals removed from abuse, neglect, or abandonment situations by law enforcement officials, like the 40 roosters police rescued from a cockfighting ring in Cleveland.

A man who was camping found Wilbur, a piglet who looked as if he had been drop-kicked like a football. Bronson the chicken was dumped on a highway in Cleveland. Barney, a logging horse for the Amish, developed a bad back and couldn't work. A piglet named Maria escaped a slaughterhouse in Mogadore. A pig named Mr. Bojangles was dumped in a school parking lot in the middle of winter.

Annette gave me a tour of the ten-acre farm. She showed me a pig tucked into a sleeping bag. Asbury had a groove around her belly left by a water hose. Someone tied it around her and never took it off. As she grew, the hose became embedded in her body and had to be removed.

I met Joy, a Holstein heifer who thinks she's a pony. At five weeks old, she was found frozen to the ground. Part of her tail broke off. It's heartbreaking until you see how Annette's heart expands for each one. She loves them back to life and finds someone to give them a permanent home.

Annette is forever grateful to Janice the pig, who changed

her life by expanding her comfort zone. Annette wears shiny pink lipstick, dark eyeliner, silver earrings, a dusty blue coat, and work boots covered in, well, you don't want to know. She's come a long way from the bridal shop, but she loves it. You might say she's in pig heaven.

There's no whining on the yacht.

Before you complain one more time about the daily grind called work, consider this: What would your life be like if you couldn't work?

We've all heard the adage "I've never met anyone on his deathbed who said, 'I wish I'd spent more time at the office.'" I used to say that until I actually met one person who vowed those won't be among the last words she utters.

All her life, all Susan wanted to do was work. When other teens were fantasizing about how they'd look in a wedding dress, she was busy visualizing herself in navy blue pumps, a plaid skirt, white blouse, blazer, and carrying a briefcase.

"A leather monogrammed briefcase," she corrected. "That's who I wanted to be. I never wanted to be somebody's mother or a traditional wife, not that there's anything wrong with those."

Susan got degrees in communications and history from Ithaca College in New York, then enrolled in graduate school in 1976 to get an MBA from the University of New Hampshire. Four weeks before graduate school started, a doctor told her she had multiple sclerosis. She was 25.

"The earth opened up and swallowed me whole, in one bite," she said, enunciating every syllable like a punch to the gut.

Her life was never the same.

When I met her she was 49 and scrunched up in a black wheelchair in her home in Shaker Heights, Ohio. She bore little resemblance to the vibrant career woman who loved shopping for briefcases and Jos. A. Bank suits with bow ties. She looked almost girlish, wearing a dandelion yellow dress, matching socks, and bright white sneakers without a scuff. Since she can no longer talk with her hands, her brown eyes and dark eyebrows leaped to punctuate her sentences.

"My limitations? I don't even know where to start. I used to be right-handed. I now eat with my left hand. I can't stand. I have home care. I cannot cut my food. I haven't been able to button my shirt since 1982," she said.

Susan can't push her own wheelchair, can't open her own mail, can't drive a car, can't pick up a pen if it falls. She paused and took stock of her abilities and delivered the summation like a punch line: "I have a big mouth and one hand.

"Look, I am not a victim. This just isn't my first choice," she clarified. "I was robbed, but life isn't fair. You do the best you can. I don't envy anybody their own life, but I wanted mine."

She did get that MBA and used it in the computer department of the Cleveland Clinic. Her parents had to come over at

6 a.m. to help dress her, then pour her into the car. At work, someone had to take her out of the car and into the office. "The people in my department were extraordinary," she says. "I never would have made it without them."

She quit working more than ten years ago when it became too difficult.

With work no longer the centerpiece of her life, Susan volunteers all over town. When asked what she missed about the world of work, a peace settled over her face like sweet memories of a lost lover.

"There was a dignity and an elegance...and pearl earrings, little ones, tasteful ones. You had authority. You were good at what you did," she said as if talking about another person. In a way, she was.

"You need someplace bigger than you to belong to. You miss the ideas, the stimulation. You miss having to decide. Work legitimizes you. I miss the connections. I miss the normal."

She offered one piece of advice for those who get to complain about rush-hour traffic, long hours, and crabby bosses: "Treasure what you have."

After meeting her, I had a new perspective on work and a renewed sense of gratitude. I wonder what our jobs would look like solely through the eyes of gratitude.

What if we all went on a gratitude binge every day, and saw everyone and everything as the gift that it really is? We probably would realize that most of us are sitting on a yacht compared to the rest of the world.

A lot of what we complain about is what someone else would love to have. That slow drive to work through rush-

.hour traffic? That arrogant boss? That annoying coworker? That small paycheck? To someone who can't work or find a job, those are all gifts.

Someone created a great video of people from third-world countries reading the complaints of people from first-world countries at www.waterislife.com. A boy sitting in a pile of dirt says, "I hate when my leather seats aren't heated." A woman standing by a river where women wash their clothes says she hates "when I leave my clothes in the washer so long that they start to smell." A boy with a goat laments, "When I leave my charger downstairs." The video ends with the words: "First-world problems are not problems."

My friend Connie always reminds me, "There's no whining on the yacht." That's where a lot of us are sitting compared to most people in the world, especially those who are unemployed and treading water. There are days when I whine about an editor making changes to my writing when I'm blessed to be paid to write for a living. There are times when I moan about the hassles of filling out a monthly mileage form when I'm lucky to get reimbursed for travel expenses.

Through the eyes of gratitude, the job you have is still worthy of praise and thanks. It might not seem like a yacht. It might look more like a small powerboat or a canoe or a life raft, but if you're employed, your head is still above water. If you keep your chin up, the view is bound to get better every day.

No one can drain you without your permission.

The gas bill to heat our old house kept getting bigger, so we decided to find out where we were losing heat so we could put more insulation in the walls to stop the leaks.

My friend Bill came over with his special infrared thermometer. It looked like a small yellow gun. Everywhere he pointed it, a red dot appeared on the wall and the temperature of the area near the red dot registered on the meter.

Bill aimed the gun at the back-door landing. The temperature near the floor was 43 degrees. Cold air was seeping in around the door. The temperature on one wall was 53. The temperature on a nearby wall was 68 degrees. The energy leaks were easy to find with that gun.

Once we found all the leaks in the house, we caulked and insulated and added weather stripping. Our budgeted gas bill dropped from $185 to $118 a month. We stayed cozy and warm all winter.

Wouldn't it be great to have a little gizmo like that to point all over your life to see where the energy sneaks out? Imagine how much more productive you could be if you could get rid of all your personal energy leaks. Imagine taking on only projects that energized you. Imagine how you would feel if you chose only friends, partners, and coworkers who fired you up instead of blowing out your pilot light.

There are some days I feel like I'm having my own personal energy crisis. Days when I can feel the life force leave me, when I catch myself saying, "I'm so overwhelmed...I'm so exhausted...I feel so drained."

I've heard it said that how you spend your energy matters more than how you spend your time. Instead of time management, people now focus on energy management.

So where does all that energy go? Once you find the leaks, you can plug them up. It didn't take me long to identify my leaks once I became willing to look for them.

I fritter away energy checking and rechecking e-mail, Facebook, and Twitter. I lose energy when I skip breakfast and lunch.

Energy pours out when I gossip, complain, criticize, blame, and doubt. Energy sneaks out when I react and give in to drama instead of waiting and thoughtfully responding to someone. It leaks out when I handle the same papers over and over and keep reshuffling them on my desk. Energy seeps out in all the unfocused and unnecessary brainstorms that clutter my thinking and my desk.

I get drained by staying up late playing sudoku or watching a movie I've seen 20 times before, like *The Proposal*, *Sweet Home Alabama*, or *My Best Friend's Wedding*. By constantly saying yes and adding more demands on my depleted self. By reading horrifying news stories that still disturb me hours later. By listening to drama that isn't mine.

I constantly try to squeeze more out of me and more onto my calendar, as if each day will expand beyond 24 hours and each week beyond 7 days. I'm not alone. We tend to respect our electronics more than our own bodies. We plug in our cell phones to recharge them every night but barely get enough sleep to recharge ourselves.

The good thing is, once you find your personal energy leaks, you can plug them up. Here's what works for me:

Prayer and meditation. The most important thing I do, every morning, is to tap into divine energy, that endless source of energy.

I post positive affirmations on my desk, car, and mirror to remind me how to be my best self.

It's important to choose the right sound track to your life. I'm a big fan of country music. It used to be so full of heartache, lying, cheating, and somebody-done-somebody-wrong songs. We used to tell this joke: What do you get when you play a country music record backward? You get your dog back, your truck back, your wife back. The country songs I listen to now fill me with hope and laughter.

Also, I try to do just one thing at a time. When I eat a meal, I eat the meal. I no longer read the paper or flip channels while eating or eat while on the Internet, iPhone, or iPad.

Fake deadlines are great. If there isn't a real deadline, I make up a fake one for myself. That way I don't waste time meandering around a project or column or book chapter for weeks or squander hours surfing the web if it's not needed.

H.A.L.T. Don't get too **h**ungry, too **a**ngry, too **l**onely, too **t**ired. My friends in recovery taught me that. Too many people skip lunch every day. They're too busy to eat. There's no such thing.

I consult my "no" coach before saying yes to another new project, brainstorm, or major commitment of time. My sister Joan helps me stay grounded in facts, not fiction, about my ability to do what I want and not what "should" be done. I love Anne Lamott's words: "I live by the truth that 'no' is a complete sentence." Amen, sister.

I'm learning to say no to my biggest time and energy drains when it comes to work:

E-mail: Instead of checking it compulsively when I don't have time to answer it (which means I'll only have to read it again), I read it once, then respond and delete.

Paperwork: How does it grow so high so fast on a desk? Someone taught me this tip: Every time you touch a piece of paper, put a staple in the corner. If you find a paper with a zillion staples, that means you're avoiding the subject of the paper. Either act on it, file it, or toss it.

Crazy-makers: Every workplace seems to have a few characters who suck up all the oxygen in the room. You feel them before you see them. They constantly create problems where none exist through gossip and envy and want you to join forces with them to defeat the imaginary enemies in their heads. Stay clear, stay sane, and stay away.

Saying yes just to please someone else: I used to suggest projects just to impress others during meetings, then left realizing I didn't have the time or the interest to complete those projects.

Procrastination: Too often I avoid the most important thing to do out of fear. The anxiety over completing it grows like a storm in my brain and the clouds of doubt keep me from getting clarity on anything else in front of me. Now I blast through the toughest thing first and get them over with.

If you can't say no, do a cost analysis of what it will mean to say yes. It always costs something, either time or energy or both. When I was getting overwhelmed giving speeches (on top of writing two columns a week, hosting a weekly radio show, and writing my next book), I consulted Joan about how to say no to some of the speaking requests. Joan listened to my concerns about how hard it was to say no to important groups and organizations and friends and family members who all had a worthy cause and wanted me to support it by being their speaker. But too much of a good thing is still too much.

My husband once said to me, "Too many chocolate bars." What? "One chocolate bar is great. Two looks better. Three is a little much. Four is too many. Five is a stomachache." Even if I could do all the talks, it wouldn't be good for me. I wouldn't be living, I'd be performing for a living.

There's only so much "you" to go around. Joan gave me a solution using simple math: What will it cost you, from door to door? Include driving time, preparation time, greeting people, signing books, thanking people, and so on. Then look at what you are giving up: time with the grandbabies, spouse, or hobbies, et cetera. Then list the benefits. For example, How many people will you touch? If it doesn't make sense to say yes but guilt is tugging at you to do so, measure the guilt factor. Draw a timeline that goes from one to ten. Mark where your guilt falls. When you do, you see clearly that you are letting guilt make your decisions and drain the life out of you. Guilt is a terrible tyrant that never lets up.

She also suggested I draw another timeline, this one to gauge my passion. Write NO on one end and YES on the other. Does saying yes to this particular task make my heart sing or my face fall? Where is the "wow"? If there is no "wow," the answer is NO. Period.

I'm not there yet, but I'd like to get better at using these, too:

Set a specific, limited amount of time to check e-mail, voice mail, Facebook, and Twitter.

Feed myself healthy, live nourishment every day instead of food that isn't actually fuel for my body, like soda, chips, and ice cream.

Spend more lunch hours with friends just to catch up, not to do business or network.

"Stop multi-tasking and start multi-asking" is a great tip from motivational speaker Colette Carlson. "The solution isn't time management. It's *you* management," she said at a conference I attended. She suggested making a not-to-do list and put down all those "shoulds." Instead of calling it selfish, focus on the *ish*: **I** stay **h**ealthy. I also like her version of a sit-down family meal. "Cereal works," she said. "Or McDonald's. They're called Happy Meals for a reason."

Stop micromanaging the husband, kids, and coworkers. I don't have to oversee every detail. No, they won't do it perfectly, which is to say, my way. They might actually do it their way, which could actually be better.

Tame the takers. Who are the takers? All those people who want more and more time. It could be your spouse, child, or boss. Whoever it is, get better at saying no. If you can't say no, practice saying "Wait." No one can drain you without your permission. Be with people who complete you, not people who deplete you. I love these words a friend e-mailed me: "No one can drive you crazy unless you give them the keys."

A friend on a retreat taught me to get my own physical flow of energy going by tapping different places on my body. You know how gorillas pound on their chests? Try it. It's incredibly energizing.

Once you figure out where you squander your energy, you can start plugging up the leaks. Once you do, you'll have more time and energy for the work and the people who matter most—starting with you.

There's more to life than making it go faster.

The poster stopped me cold: *Never confuse having a career with having a life.*

It doesn't matter what we do for a living if we don't take time to have a life.

Sometimes the best thing you can do for yourself and others is to hit the brakes and slow down. I'm all for more downtime. There's an actual International Day of Leisure to celebrate it. Every year I miss it. I'm too busy.

It's a great idea to take a day off to pause, reflect, and have fun. How about a season of leisure? Wait. Isn't that what summer is supposed to be?

Life flies by so fast, you wonder, Did someone speed up the rotation of the earth? Short-sheet the calendar? The way we live, you would think one of the Ten Commandments was "Thou shalt not rest."

Even God took a day to rest.

Most of us don't.

Whether you honor the Sabbath on Saturday or Sunday, it used to be a time to silence the noise. Albert Schweitzer once advised people not to let the Sabbath be taken away, that if your soul doesn't have a Sabbath, it becomes an orphan.

We are a nation of orphans.

Our kids play in baseball, soccer, and hockey leagues on the Sabbath. Our stores sell liquor and beer during sermons. Our malls, grocery stores, convenience stores, and strip centers fill with shoppers. When I was a kid, you couldn't find a gas station open on the Sabbath and most stores were closed to honor the commandment "Remember the Sabbath day, to keep it holy."

We'd go to church, come home, and sit down for a big family meal. We didn't call them sit-down dinners; it was a given that we sat around the dining room table and didn't get up until everyone finished. If the phone rang, it was treated like a misdemeanor. "Tell them to call back. We're eating," my dad would bark.

Then we would spend the afternoon visiting Uncle Joe or driving out to see Grandma and Grandpa on the farm. We would snap beans. We would press blades of long grass between our thumbs and whistle. We would eat tomatoes and cucumbers warm off the vine. No one was in a hurry. There was nowhere to go because nothing was open.

Now the Sabbath day is just another day. People run errands, shop, and work. They're getting too busy to read the Sunday paper. Whatever happened to a day of rest?

We fill Sunday with work and projects. We boast about

what great type A's we are all the way to the cardiac-care unit. We talk incessantly about our multitasking until we suddenly remember that we forgot to pick up the kids from soccer.

We overschedule our kids, bragging about how many sports leagues Jason plays in and how many classes Bethany attends to learn ballet, gymnastics, German, and piano before she starts kindergarten. We're teaching our kids multitasking. We're teaching them to fill up every weekend, to postpone joy until retirement.

When was the last time your kids played a game of capture the flag? Spent a night on the front stoop studying the stars? When was the last time they caught lightning bugs? Climbed a tree? Read a comic book? Had a grass fight? Ran through a sprinkler? Have you ever taken them fishing? For a walk to get ice cream? In the woods exploring?

If we don't teach them the fine art of wasting time, who will?

What if we stopped scheduling every minute and let them be bored long enough to discover their own imaginations? We might also discover our own.

If you've already got a strong work ethic, it's time to strengthen your play ethic. Forget about where fun fits in your five-year plan. Where does it fit in your five-hour plan?

A while back an anonymous e-mail made the rounds with advice on how to maintain a healthy level of insanity. It suggested putting your trash can on your desk and labeling it "In." Skip instead of walk. Wrap mosquito netting around your cubicle and play tropical sounds all day.

Why not add to the list? Stick a drink umbrella in your coffee at work, kick off your shoes and go barefoot in your cubicle. When you get home after a long day, sit in a hammock and appoint yourself in charge of Cloud Patrol.

Unplug the TV. Turn off the computer. Confiscate all cell phones, video games, and iPads. Kick the kids out of the house. Kick yourself out, too.

Round up the neighbors for a game of flashlight tag. Hold a scavenger hunt, a pet show, a talent show. Play charades on the front lawn. Make musical instruments out of clutter from the kitchen and garage. Don't lecture the kids on how great it was back when you were a kid. Get out and show them.

Don't call it downtime.

It's called living.

Instead of planning a better life, start living one.

One day I was having a pity party that no one else attended but me. My writing was at a standstill. A finished manuscript sat on my desk, but I was too scared to send it to an agent or publisher for fear it would be rejected. I wanted to know God's perfect path before I'd take one wobbly step down the wrong road.

My husband said, "You're looking for a sign, but the sign is in you. It's up to you. You haven't done anything to get it published. You haven't taken any action. You keep waiting for God to tell you what to do. Maybe I am your sign: send the book out."

I did, and I'm still stunned that it ended up in 26 countries.

An old Amish guy used to tell me, "You can pray for potatoes, but grab a hoe." One of my friends in recovery used to say, "God will do for us what we cannot do for ourselves, but God won't do for us what we're supposed to do."

Most of us don't procrastinate because we're lazy. We delay action because we're afraid of taking the wrong step, so we don't take any step.

It's like the guy who prayed to God again and again to win the lottery, but he never did. One day in the middle of that prayer, he heard God's booming voice yell down from heaven, "Buy a ticket!"

If you want to win the lottery, buy a ticket. If you want potatoes, you can pray all you want, but you'd better grab a hoe. You can have faith in God, but you have to back it up with action, even the smallest bit of action. You have to do what you can do.

Part of me rebels and resists action. I want a better moment, a perfect story line delivered from beginning to end before any word is typed. I want assurance that this is the right idea from the start all the way to the end. How can I act before I'm ready? But maybe there is no "ready."

I often fool myself into thinking I am actually taking action when I'm only planning and organizing and reading about taking action. I've bought countless books on how to exercise and have read them all without stretching a muscle.

Whenever I want to learn something new, I take a class or read a book instead of just jumping in and doing it. I once read four books on how to play piano better. I put all my notes in a three-ring binder. Did I play any scales or songs? Nope. Not a note.

So many people who tell me they want to be writers take endless classes and go to countless conferences but won't move a pen. It's safer to stay in the dream of writing a play or novel and enjoy all the possibilities instead of trying them out and failing. I admire people who are willing to risk doing something imperfectly instead of perfectly doing nothing.

One of the prayers I heard on a retreat included these words: "I have spent my life, Lord, tuning up my lyre instead of singing to You." My guess is God just wants to hear us sing, even if we're off-key. Father Clem Metzger was a director at the Jesuit Retreat House. I savor this precious moment when he asked a woman to do a reading for Mass. She looked scared as she reviewed the Bible verse. Then she asked him for help on how to pronounce a few words beforehand. "Oh, stumble through it," he told her.

Stumble through it.

What great advice.

We're all stumbling through life. Some of us are just better at covering it up.

I once attended a retreat where Dr. Francoise Adan gave a talk called "Bringing Peace Inside Out." She was born in Italy and grew up in Belgium. She got her medical degree and decided to specialize in helping people take care of their minds, bodies, and spirits. She is co–medical director of the Connor Integrative Medicine Network at University Hospitals and assistant professor at Case Western Reserve University Medical School. People call her a wellness champion. I can see why.

The room was packed with busy women who took a day off, but many were cheating, tapping away on BlackBerry devices and iPhones under the table. She urged all of us to cease our endless doing. First she had us breathe, and make our exhale longer than our inhale. Breathe in four counts, breathe out six counts.

Then she had us pose this question to ourselves: *What will most benefit my well-being?*

The room fell silent. What came to me was this: Stop planning and start living. What would it take for me to trust life and embrace it 100 percent right here and now? What if I could let go of the quest for perfection and believe that completion, not perfection, is good enough?

That quest to live life perfectly keeps me from actually living. I overthink. I plan too much. I organize too much.

Then she had us all participate in an exercise I'll never forget. She held up a feather boa and described feathers as light and airy, versus goals, which are weighty and bog us down. She asked us to picture a set of scales with what we wanted to do on one side and what we didn't want to do on the other side. Instead of burying ourselves under the burden of endless goals, what if we just did one action, one feather-sized bit of action? If you add a feather to the scale, it doesn't make much difference at first, until you add another, then another.

Just one feather will tip the balance in your favor. What is your feather? Your one thing that will tip the scale? What is your feather today?

She passed the boa around the room and had us each pluck one feather off and share what feather, what action, we were going to take or stop taking to change our lives.

One by one by one, we took turns and shared our feathers. Women resolved to reach out to friends, to write down one thing they appreciate about themselves, to ask for help, to leave work by six every night. They vowed to check e-mails less often, go to yoga, hire a personal trainer, schedule half an hour of "me" time on the work calendar. They announced they would set time for margaritas with girlfriends, morning affirmations, and naps.

I left the retreat with a simple blue feather and a vow to stop putting more on my to-do list. And what I do add to that list has to be worthy of my life, because that's what my time is—my life.

The world needs people who are fully alive.

Always saddle your own horse.

I thought of that cowgirl's motto as I tugged at the leather straps, making them as tight as possible so I wouldn't fall. This was no horse, but to me, it was just as scary.

After reading an obituary on Connie Douglas Reeves, the country's oldest cowgirl, I decided it was time to get busy living. The Texan cowgirl, who was 101, hard of hearing, and nearly blind, died after her horse, Dr Pepper, threw her.

Amazing. She was still on a horse at 101.

Too many of us never even get on one. We live life too carefully. We're afraid of getting hurt. I used to think the best way to die was to grow old, fall asleep, and never wake up. The cowgirl changed my mind. Don't tiptoe to death. Go out with a bang. Go out living.

Not that I planned to go out anytime soon, but I did plan to go up. About 800 feet in the sky, strapped in a powered parachute that looks like an industrial fan attached to a go-kart fitted with two seats and a parachute.

I had just finished reading yet another book that urged me to get out of my comfort zone, to feel the fear and do it anyway, when my friend Hal Becker called. He'd been calling for weeks leaving chirpy messages on the answering machine: "The weather's just right...Looks gorgeous out...Call me."

I wanted to go up—well, I wanted *to want* to go up—but I don't even go on Ferris wheels, cable cars, or roller coasters. But because of that dang cowgirl, I said yes.

Nothing stopped her. Internet stories told how she would brand cattle, castrate sheep, and kill rattlesnakes. She broke her leg in '86 when a horse kicked her. A horse threw her after riding into a hornet's nest when she was 91. She broke her wrist and five ribs and punctured a lung.

She once told an Associated Press reporter about her sister-in-law, who was a decade younger, wasting away watching TV. The cowgirl grumbled, "What kind of living is that? You have to get out in the world and look at all the wonderful things."

That's what Hal promised. A wonderful view.

I trusted Hal's view of the world.

Hal Becker was diagnosed with stage 3 cancer at 28. They gave him three months to live. The testicular cancer had already spread to his abdomen, chest, and brain. That was back in 1983. He carries a photo of himself when he weighed 83 pounds and had burn marks on his arms from the chemotherapy.

He became an author, sales training guru, and international speaker. But he plays as hard as he works. Maybe harder. Being a cancer survivor, he knows there are no guarantees about having a long life, so he has the time of his life all the time. He plays in a band, takes aerial photography, and soaks up every sunset he can from the sky. He makes the most out of now. As he says, "Now will never come again."

How could I say no to Hal? As we stood in a high school football field, Hal tossed a handful of grass into the air to check the wind, grinned, and said, "It's a great night for flying."

He unpacked the rainbow nylon parachute, untangled the strings (mere strings!) attached to the go-kart, then handed me a helmet.

"Anything in your front pockets?" he asked, not wanting anything to fall into the propeller. I quickly dumped out the contents of my pockets.

I tightened the straps of the shoulder harness, put on the helmet, and took a deep breath. Hal climbed into the front seat and we bounced along the grass on three small tires. Suddenly, we were floating on air.

Hal warned me that the first minute might "disorient" me. I'd have used the word *terrorize*. But he was right. After a minute, my body got used to the rush of wind around me, the feeling that there was nothing to hold on to, yet nothing to fear.

We floated over lush treetops, blue swimming pools, emerald ponds, brown slivers of deer, and into the setting sun. When we landed gently on the grass, Hal asked, "Do you feel it?"

Some would call it a rush of adrenaline. I think it's something else. A flush of joy running through every vein. I bet it's how that cowgirl felt after every ride. She'd told reporters she'd never quit. "It's in my blood."

She wasn't talking about riding. She was talking about living.

One way to jump-start your life is to write your obituary and live it while you're alive. That's what Nancy Lee Hixson did. I never met her, but I wished I had after reading her obituary that ran in the *Plain Dealer* where I work.

She actually wrote her own obituary and kept revising it for seven years. Nancy packed as much life as she could into her 65. She died at sunrise on June 30, 2009. Here's what she had to say about her life. Her family said it was all true:

In addition to being a tee-totaling mother and an indifferent housekeeper...she often volunteered as an ombudsman to help disadvantaged teens find college funding and early opened her home to many children of poverty, raising several of them to successful, if unwilling, adulthood.

She also enjoyed a long life of unmentionable adventures and confessed she had been a rebellious teen-aged library clerk, an untalented college student on scholarship, a run-away hippie, a stoic Sunday school teacher, a Brownie leader, a Grange lecturer, an expert rifleman, a waitress, a wife once or twice, a welder, an artist, and a writer.

She was the CEO of the Cuyahoga Valley Center of Outdoor Leadership Training, where she lived in a remote and tiny one-room cabin in the Cuyahoga Valley National Park. Despite the lack of cabin space and dining table, she often served holiday dinners to friends and relatives and could seat twenty at the bed.

She lived the last twenty-three years at Winter Spring Farm near Danville, Ohio, where she built a private Stonehenge, and planted and helped save from extinction nearly 50 varieties of antique apple trees. Her homemade cider and wine were reputed to cause sudden stupor.

She befriended countless stray dogs, cats, horses, and the occasional goat. She was a nemesis to hunters, and an activist of unpopular, but just, causes. In short, she did all things enthusiastically, but nothing well. After moving to Danville, she bravely suffered with a severe and disabling disorder and a ten-year battle with lymphoma that ultimately took her life.

She was often confined to the home where she continued to tirelessly volunteer and donate her limited resources to needy teens in the area, always cheered by their small and large achievements. Sympathy and big donations may be extended at this time.

After listing the survivors, Nancy's obituary read, "She was a long-time card carrying member of the ACLU, the Democratic Party, and of MENSA. In lieu of flowers, please pray for the Constitution of the United States."

What a life.

It reminded me of that powerful quote by Howard Thurman, who said: "Don't ask what the world needs. Ask what makes you come alive, and go do it. Because what the world needs is people who have come alive."

What makes you come alive?

It might not be work. It could be everything else that surrounds it.

The best use of your life is to love.

My daughter married a man who grew up with 63 brothers and sisters.

His parents, Elsie and Kevin Sullivan, had 3 children but were foster parents to 60 babies.

They made a career out of loving other people's children. They were emergency foster parents for babies who were taken from parents because of abuse, neglect, or medical emergencies. I can't even begin to imagine all the diapers and feedings and fevers they soothed. My son-in-law got a PhD in love in that house.

I once interviewed a boy who wanted to be adopted. There's still a huge crack in my heart from Maurice. I met him years ago, when he was 12, when he was running out of hope. He knew he was running out of childhood. He knew that most people wanted a baby or a toddler to adopt. Still, he got excited when his picture ran in the *Plain Dealer*'s weekly feature, "A Child Waits." His personal ad seeking new parents described him as a bright, creative, artistic boy who was in residential treatment for abuse and neglect, who wanted at the time to be the first black president of the United States.

Only no one called.

Maurice was old enough to know that no one wanted him.

"It's kind of hard to be patient when years just flow by," he said softly. "Why won't anybody call?"

What would he say to someone who would consider taking him? He grinned so wide his huge cheeks squeezed his eyes into black slits holding onyx jewels. "Come on," he said, sounding like a salesman. "You're making a good choice. It's an opportunity you can't miss!"

From a kid's point of view, it's easy to feel like you're being punished for your parents' mistakes when no one wants to adopt you. The anger takes over, you act up, and then it's even harder for someone to want you. When I met Maurice, he was living with 42 children at Beech Brook in Pepper Pike, Ohio. He had been there the longest—going on two years. I asked him how many foster homes he'd had.

"Whoa," he said as he did the math. "Twelve, at least."

Maurice was taken from his parents when he was seven. His two sisters ended up in foster homes. He wished he were in one, even though they scared him.

"You get all nervous," he said, wringing his hands. "You don't really know anybody. You don't know where the kitchen is, where the bathroom is. It's kind of like first being born. You don't know what it's going to be like."

And you never know how long you will last there. He

thought the last foster parents would keep him. "They said they wanted to adopt me," he said. "I guess I just jinxed myself."

He talked dreamily about how he got to play hide-and-seek there, and how on the day he left, they threw him a party and his foster mom cried. "I don't even remember the phone number or address," he said, staring at his sneakers.

Before getting therapy, Maurice disrupted foster homes. In time, he learned not to throw a chair or swear when he was angry, but to talk about why he was upset. His history scares people from seeing who he is now and who he could be.

He did have one piece of hope to cling to. Maurice had a mentor to help him practice his new skills in the real world. Dave, an archaeologist with the Cleveland Museum of Art, took him out every Saturday.

"He's delightful," David told me. "He's real smart and fun to be with. He's dying for affection. He'd get along with anybody."

Before the mentor came along, Maurice felt hopeless. He told his therapist, "I don't want to live anymore. I'd be better off in heaven." Maurice wasn't choosy about the kind of family he wanted. "I want a family that doesn't do drugs, that's nonviolent," he told me.

It was hard for him to see other kids get adopted and leave. Each time that happened, the hurt deepened.

"Man, everybody is leaving me," Maurice said, shaking his head. "Every time my best friend leaves, I just try to make another best friend."

As far as I know, Maurice never got adopted and aged out

of the system. I don't know where he is, but he has a heart full of hurt. He's not the only one. I once interviewed a group of children at a camp for kids who were getting too old to adopt. They were 13 to 17 years old, and they talked about the Good Life, back when they had dads and moms, brothers and sisters, bedrooms and backyards that never changed.

They talked about when they got the bad news. A parent died or got arrested and wasn't coming back. They talked of how they reacted to the news. Some screamed. One threw up. Another couldn't speak. One confided, "I still can't believe it." They talked about the anger of leaving behind younger siblings and friends; about not being told a sister was adopted until a year later; about being watched constantly in foster homes; about cousins, aunts, uncles who never called or came for them.

They shared the bargaining they tried: *If I get straight As, if I behave, if I'm quiet, maybe then I can go back home.* Each one shared how they didn't feel good enough for anyone to love them. The camp volunteer had each one light a candle to remind them they could still choose hope and that no one else could make that light go out. She wanted them to reach a place of acceptance that they might never return to the Good Life, but they could create a new one.

If only there were more people like Jean and Chuck Harrell, who offer children a new life. They've been married for nearly 60 years and have taken in 300 children. Loving other people's children became their mission in life. They call it their ministry. It was her idea.

"We had to pray a *lot*," she said.

They had three of their own children, then decided to become foster parents. Any resistance Chuck might have had, Jean prayed it away.

One day he said, "Okay, let's do it," and they've never stopped.

When I last spoke to them, he was 81, she was 78.

What a journey it has been.

They've had nine children living in their home in tiny Rootstown, Ohio, a town with two traffic lights. Their home became an oasis for children who had been abused and neglected. One time they took in an entire family at a moment's notice. The family was driving through from another state when they were in a car accident. The parents ended up in the hospital; the children ended up at Jean and Chuck's. The day the children were to leave, one of the boys went exploring at the park down the road. He discovered an outhouse, took a look inside, and fell in. He came back a stinking mess. Jean had to hurry to clean him up before his aunt arrived.

"We just laughed," Jean said.

And sometimes they cried.

"They come in with problems. Some are medical, some are physical, some are behavioral," Jean said.

All the children have touched them, but a little guy named Isaac left the deepest mark. One day the county children services called and asked them to take a baby. He had been shaken and his brain was badly damaged. Jean and Chuck went to the hospital to see the baby to decide whether they could care for him. They were told the baby probably wouldn't live. They decided to take the baby anyway.

"The only instruction they gave us was who to call when the baby died," Jean said.

They just poured love all over him, every moment they could.

"We prayed and prayed and worked as hard as we could with the baby," she said.

Isaac had lost part of his vision. He couldn't talk or sit. He had endless doctor appointments. They had to feed him through a tube, take him to physical therapy, give him medicine all day. His immune system was so weak, they gave up going to church so they wouldn't expose him to harm.

"That baby was God's special child and God didn't mind us missing church," she said. "We were doing what the Lord wanted us to do."

"All he could do is lay on his back, but he had the most beautiful smile you ever saw," Jean said. "He'd wave his arms and legs and coo. He was the happiest baby."

He could still feel love. That's what saved him. Their love.

They had him for almost three years. He left when another family adopted him.

"He was just pure joy," Jean said.

And now he is someone else's joy.

To find out who you are, let go of who you aren't.

If you grew up watching the TV game show *Let's Make a Deal*, you know how hard it is to choose the right door.

Contestants on the show are given the option to trade in a prize they have already won, like a TV or an oven, for what is behind door number 1, 2, or 3. They usually gamble all their winnings for one of those mysteries, even though a booby prize waits behind one mystery door.

What's behind door number 1? It could be a trip to Hawaii, a luxury car, or a dining room set. Or it could be a donkey, a jalopy, or a year's supply of furniture polish.

In real life, we usually want to cling to what we know and have for as long as we can. Too often when one door closes, we stand at that door and keep pounding away on it, as if more noise and effort will force it open. Meanwhile, another door might be unlocked or even standing wide open, but we refuse to budge from the closed one.

For years, I hosted a public affairs radio show on an NPR affiliate in Cleveland. I loved doing radio. I loved it so much I hosted for free every Friday during the 9 a.m. hour. But in time, I ached to do more topics that focused on the heart and soul, on topics I call "internal" affairs. So I wrote up a plan to create an entire radio show called *Internal Affairs*. I listed page after page of topic ideas for the show. I couldn't wait to present it to management.

No one wanted it.

No one.

Instead, they wanted to tighten the focus of the existing show even more on topics related to business, the economy, and politics. None of those topics made my heart sing or my passion meter fly off the scale. One week we did a show on auto industry workers but our guests were analysts for the car industry, not real live auto workers, which is what I suggested.

One week I was given the choice to do a show on Asian carp in Lake Erie or the building of the Innerbelt Bridge. I chose the bridge and hosted a rousing discussion, but it wasn't a topic I would have tuned in to as a listener.

That's when I knew I was the proverbially square peg trying to fit into a round hole. I should be hosting shows I actually wanted to listen to, and management should be presenting shows they believed in. We were no longer a match. It was time to go. So I left.

What to do with my big brainstorm? I took it to another nearby public radio station. WKSU-FM loved it. They gave me my own weekly show, *The Regina Brett Show*. I found my match. The tagline was: "Smart...with heart." They kept telling me, "Be you. We want more of you in the show." More of me? Wow. That's clarity. That's how I knew I was in the right place.

Sometimes the slam of one door reverberates so loudly in our ears it's hard to hear the quiet opening of the next door. We often hear the quote "When God closes one door He opens another." We rarely hear the words that follow it. Helen Keller added another important part when she said when one door of happiness closes, another opens; but instead of walking through it, we stand stuck at the closed door and miss seeing the one that has swung open for us.

Sometimes we have to let go of who we are to find out who we are being called to be. We have to give up the good for the great. My friend Adam Shapiro traded the good for the great. He was at the top of his game in Cleveland with a coveted spot as the anchor of WEWS-TV's (ABC) show *Good Morning Cleveland*. He did the early evening newscast called "Live on Five." He won awards for his work as an anchor and a reporter.

His friends—including me—were stunned when he quit that plum job and headed for the Big Apple. He didn't go there for a job. He went there for the possibility of one. He always wanted to live in New York City. He ended up being a general assignment reporter in New York for the WNBC-TV morning show *Today in New York*, then landed a job at FOX Business Network.

Midlife crisis?

Not at all. He called it a midlife correction.

Sometimes life corrects your life for you. For years, my column ran on the front of the Metro section. But I had gradually quit writing local metro columns about crime and corruption to focus on columns that would uplift and inspire. They say,

"Success is doing most what you do best." It was time to do my best work, the work I felt most passionate about.

I came in one day excited about my new book *Be the Miracle*, a collection of inspirational essays. I brought signed copies for each editor. When I handed one to the managing editor, he asked me to sit down. He broke the news that my column was being moved. He said it no longer fit the local metro page. It would go on page A-2. It knocked the wind out of me for a few seconds. Oh, no, my writing would no longer be on a section front, the prime real estate in the newspaper. Then I realized, *Wait a minute, this is a gift*.

A new door was opening. Behind this new door, I was free to write more inspirational columns and wasn't limited by local news. I would no longer be expected to write commentaries about crime and corruption. I was free once I released my old job with this prayer:

"God, thank You for all You have given me, thank You for all You have taken, but mostly, thank You for what You have left me."

I see myself now as an inspirational writer, not a journalist. No more apologizing for who I am or for who I am not. I'm getting better at saying no to what I know clearly isn't my calling. If there's no joy in it, no smile in it, it's not mine to do.

You don't have to be good at everything. If you try to be, you'll probably end up mediocre at everything. Leo Buscaglia used to tell a great story about why we should treasure our uniqueness. He told how the animals got together and created a school. To paraphrase his story, each animal played a part in designing the curriculum. The rabbit wanted running on the curriculum, the bird wanted flying on it, the fish wanted swimming, and the squirrel wanted perpendicular tree climbing.

What happened next? Everyone was expected to excel at everything, which ruined everything for everybody. The rabbit was great at running, but fell out of the tree trying to climb it and got injured. That hurt his running, so when it came report card time, he no longer got As in running and he flunked tree climbing. The bird broke a wing trying to burrow in the ground and ended up with a C in flying and flunked burrowing.

The moral of the story for me is this: If you try to be a second-rate version of someone else, you will fail to be a first-rate version of you. All God wants for me to be is me, the very thing I hold back because I believe I'm not worthy. God already knows that and doesn't care.

Whenever I feel like an oddity in the world of journalism, I read this e-mail a reader sent me. Paul wrote it after reading a column I wrote about a soldier who died. At his funeral, his daughter carried his Purple Heart:

Dear Ms. Brett, Each person is born with a gift from God. Some people can cook, really knock your tongue out. Some sew or woodwork. Some people are natural born Mommies, that know when to wipe a tear or bake a pie. You my friend, can paint. I have never considered the keyboard the tool of an artisan, and yet, in your hands, a picture is painted of an event, or an every day occurrence that becomes a piece of the heart of the person reading it.

Your capabilities of reaching out and plucking exactly

the right heartstring is astounding to me. You pierced me today. Understand that the gifts I mentioned from God are not ours to possess. They are meant to be shared to make life whole and fuller for as many others as possible. In my opinion, God is well pleased with your use and sharing of his gift.

When I stop trying to be someone else and settle for being me, great things come to pass for me and for others. I love this quote: "In a world where you can be anything, be you."

Just be you. That's all God is calling you to be. And that's always enough.

Align yourself first, then take action.

It was a rough day at archery.

My arrows were flying everywhere except where I wanted them to go: smack in the center of the bull's-eye where the tiny X is.

I stood with my recurve bow in hand, quiver full of arrows, aiming for the center of the yellow bull's-eye 18 meters away. Each time I drew back the string, had my sight on the target, and it felt right to let go, I scored well. But every time the shot didn't feel right, instead of putting the bow down and starting my shot over, I fired anyway. I let go even though I heard the word *Stop* in my head. Each time, the arrows landed far from the inner circle. Damn. Why was it so hard to shoot today? Shot after shot made me more frustrated.

A woman a few archers down kept hitting the bull's-eye. From the looks of her target, it was as easy as breathing.

She even hit the X. Twice. In a row. What did she know that I didn't? What secret technique was she using? I had to find out.

After taking my three shots, I studied her. She stood at the shooting line, drew back, paused, then stopped and set the bow back down. Again and again, she put the bow down without releasing the arrow. That's the one thing I resisted doing. She stopped herself, got realigned, and started over. That's how she hit so many bull's-eyes. She never once let go of the arrow until she knew she was aligned.

We both knew when we weren't ready. One of us listened and got realigned. The other one, me, shot anyway.

In archery, they say every shot starts with your feet. Your stance has to be right before your shooting will be. Before any action is taken, you need consistent alignment. You want your body to develop muscle memory. In archery, you learn to shoot well by repetition. You find out what works, then keep repeating the same steps over and over until your body remembers them. You no longer have to think about your shot; your body just does it. And once you release the shot and it hits the target, you're supposed to forget about it, clear your mind, and get ready to shoot the next one.

You are storing and releasing energy into the bow, which then releases it into the arrow. The best archers visualize each shot; they see it before they release an arrow. They practice alignment first, then action. When I remember that and practice it, my score is higher and I have more fun shooting.

It's true about life, too.

When I am aligned, when I am spiritually centered, emotionally calm, and mentally focused, nothing rocks me. When

I'm not aligned, the smallest speed bump will knock me off balance, the smallest insult will crush me.

How do I stay aligned? Mostly through daily prayer and meditation. I call them spiritual exercises. They build muscle memory so you always know your true center and aim in life when life surprises you. Once you're aligned, in life and in archery, it's a lot easier to hit your target, because you actually know what you're aiming for.

When I worked at the *Beacon Journal* as a reporter, some editor decided we all needed to get more focused in our writing. The paper instituted a rule that every time you turned in a story, you had to write a two-sentence summary at the top of it to help the headline writers choose their words. When you think about it, the headline is the most vital part of the story. It attracts people to read it or to turn away.

At first I grumbled and resisted writing that stupid two-sentence assignment. Then I grew to love it. When I got lost writing long columns or stories, I'd often go back to the top and consult those two sentences to make sure I hadn't lost my focus. It helped me trim away the nonessential information that didn't advance the story or serve the reader.

Companies do the same thing by writing a mission statement. It serves as a compass point so everyone travels in the same direction, from CEO to secretary.

My husband once owned a PR firm whose motto was "We build relationships." His business card was the most confusing one I'd ever seen. It listed everything they did: government relations, community relations, public relations, media relations, business relations. He did so many things, no one, not even his kids or I, knew exactly what he did for a living. His "elevator speech" was fine, as long as you were going from the lobby to the 32nd floor and had 20 minutes for him to explain his line of work.

Once he decided to specialize in one thing, crisis communications, his business took off. If you try to be all things to all people, you end up not mattering much to anyone. When you do one thing and do it well, you make yourself essential.

It helps to have a focal point to keep you centered on what that one thing is. When I hosted my own radio show for three years, I didn't want to lose sight of what I wanted *The Regina Brett Show* to be. To help me stay focused on my personal mission, no matter what the topic or guests were, I wrote my own Ten Commandments for the show:

1. Be interesting. Surprise the listener.
2. Be original.
3. Be you. Sound 100 percent like Regina Brett.
4. Have fun.
5. Ask the tough questions in a respectful manner.
6. Honor the listener first.
7. Inspire all involved to find and use their inner power to create a greater life for themselves and others.
8. Give people hope.
9. Work as a team to do only what we can do well and consistently.
10. Do the best you can every week, 100 percent, then release it.

Before we started the show each week, I went into the restroom and got aligned. I held my hands together in prayer, touched them to my forehead, and asked God to bless all my thoughts with clarity; then touched my hands to my mouth and asked God to bless all my words with compassion; then touched my hands to my heart and asked God to bless my guests, staff, and listeners. Once I aligned myself, I no longer worried about what happened next.

My friend Terry Pluto is a sports columnist who also writes a column on faith for the *Plain Dealer*. We also worked together at the *Beacon Journal* many years ago. He used to write the most powerful columns about his dad, who spent his life working in a warehouse, then retired and had a stroke that left him unable to walk and barely able to talk. All he could do was grunt or say one word: "man."

Terry came on my radio show and told a powerful story about his dad, himself, and the importance of staying spiritually aligned. In 1998, Terry spent a few days with his dad in Florida and had helped him leave the hospital and get settled back home. A caretaker took over after Terry had to go back home to Akron.

Terry was supposed to go to Japan that February to cover the Winter Olympics as a sportswriter. It's a big honor for any sportswriter and a big commitment for a newspaper to make. The paper had already bought the airline ticket and paid for the accommodations. Before Terry left for the airport, he called the caretaker. Everything was the same. On the drive to the airport, Terry was praying for his dad when he heard a voice say, "Don't go."

It was as clear as if someone had said it out loud. The words stuck with him; so much so, he pulled over and called the caretaker to check on his dad. Everything was fine. Terry closed his eyes and prayed for clarity. He heard those same words, "Don't go." So he called his boss at the newspaper and said he didn't think he should go to Japan. It was an awkward call to make, since his dad was the same as before, wasn't in the hospital or near death's door, and the paper had spent thousands of dollars to send Terry there. Terry told his boss he just didn't feel good about leaving. The boss said, Don't go.

Terry drove back home and called his dad before going to bed. Terry talked to his dad, who just said his usual, "Man, man." Terry fell asleep.

At 4 a.m. his brother called. Their father had died.

I think Terry heard God speak because he constantly aligns himself to hear God. He practices prayerful listening, so when God does speak, he hears. Those two words, "Don't go," could have easily been drowned out by the noise of busy thoughts if he hadn't been aligned.

Aligning myself every morning in meditation is the best thing I do for me. One day I was just about to merge onto the interstate from the on-ramp when I heard a voice say, "Stop!" I hesitated for a brief second and then hit the brake. Good thing. Just then, a semitruck flew past. It had been in my blind spot. Had I sped ahead, I would have been crushed.

Another day I was driving down the road with too many to-do items buzzing through my brain. What should I do first? Then I looked up and saw the license plate in front of me: BE CLEAR.

It doesn't get any clearer than that.

The most important boss to answer to is the small, still voice within.

Have you ever worked for an arrogant boss?

Who hasn't?

There's actually a scale created to measure how arrogant your boss is. It's called the Workplace Arrogance Scale, WARS for short.

Stanley Silverman is an industrial and organizational psychologist at the University of Akron. Every time he asks a roomful of people, "Have you ever worked with an arrogant boss?" every hand goes up. I wonder how many of those hands belong to bosses who don't realize *they're* the arrogant ones.

Think your boss is off the scale?

Now you can verify it. Stanley and researchers at Michigan State University developed the scale after interviewing hundreds of people and collecting all the traits they saw in their bosses as arrogant.

According to the scale, your boss is arrogant if he or she: Makes decisions that impact others without listening to their input. Glares or stares to make people uncomfortable. Criticizes or belittles. Shoots down other people's ideas in public. Makes unrealistic time demands on others. Here are a few things the rest of us would add: Yells. Curses. Blames. Shames. Acts omnipotent, invincible, superior.

Everyone has a bad-boss story. I once had a boss who made one worker sit in a closet to work to punish her for being slow. The boss would order us not to talk to the woman. It was degrading for everyone. The poor woman was doing her best to keep up.

Early in my journalism career, I worked at a newspaper where we learned from a competing newspaper that our paper was for sale. We lost confidence in the owner of the paper when we realized he had no confidence in us. He held a staff meeting in the newsroom and told the roomful of journalists, "You can't believe everything you read in the paper." Great. We reporters were working for a newspaper publisher who didn't trust reporters.

Some bosses like to micromanage. I'm rarely productive for that kind of boss. I want to crawl out of my skin when I see them coming. I feel suffocated in every conversation and want to scream, "Just leave me alone and let me do my work!"

Some bosses want to correct your work before you're even finished with it. In one newsroom, one editor read electronically over my shoulder. I was typing away on a story at my desk and sent her the final version. She sent an e-mail commenting on the earlier versions, the ones I had deleted. It turns out she had been reading my writing from her computer without my knowing it. It was like Big Brother was watching.

One editor took joy in deleting my most poetic lines. He earned the nickname Captain Strike Through. Before he even read through the whole story, he started making changes in your copy. What a contrast to one of the best editors I ever had, Stuart Warner. He created a whole new model of what an editor, and a boss, could be. Whenever I turned in a story, he read it all the way through, made a few suggestions, then he got out of his chair and invited me to sit there. Together, we made the changes, but it was my hand making them. What a difference. Every story improved with his delicate touch.

It took me a long time to believe I could trust a boss. I haven't always been the easiest person to work with. I used to have a bumper sticker over my desk that read: QUESTION AUTHORITY. And, boy, did I.

For the longest time I hated any authority over me. Every boss became the father I couldn't please, and my dad was tough to please. No matter what I did growing up, it was never good enough for him, and he let me know with his belt or his rage. His constant refrain still reverberates through my head: *What the hell is wrong with you? Can't you do anything right?* My guess is he heard that from his own dad his whole childhood. As they say, when you know better, you do better. My dad just didn't know better.

If you haven't resolved your dad or mom authority issues, every boss becomes that unpleasable, unpleasant parent. One day at work a coworker was having a tough time with the boss. She complained to a reporter next to her that nothing she did could please him. The reporter laughed and said, "Daddy doesn't love you. Get over it."

It has taken me a long time to trust that every boss isn't out to punish me. To this day, if the boss asks, "Do you have a second?" my heart races and I fear the worst: *What did I do wrong? How am I going to be punished?*

It doesn't help when that is what happens. One day many years ago, the editor wanted to see me. Before walking into his office, I paused and prayed and reminded myself that it could actually be for something good, like a raise. It wasn't. Someone had written a nasty letter about my work and the editor called me into his office to tell me he was going to run it. He didn't go to bat for me; he didn't have my back. I left feeling battered and bruised, which is how I felt as a child.

When I left my job as a columnist at the *Beacon Journal* to become a columnist at the *Plain Dealer*, I gave myself a fresh start. I figured it would be easy. I was already a columnist; I knew how to write, how to meet deadlines, and had already won national writing awards. So why did I get hit with a wave of anxiety a week before I started my new job? It made no sense. I would be doing the same job, just for new people.

Bingo. Would I be able to please that new boss? It hit the old childhood button: fear of Dad's disapproval. Then a friend in recovery shared this passage from the "Big Book" of Alcoholics Anonymous. It gave me a new perspective on who's really boss. The passage describes AA's third step:

Made a decision to turn our will and our lives over to the care of God as we understood Him...

We decided that hereafter in this drama of life, God

was going to be our Director. He is the Principal; we are His agents. He is the Father, and we are His children… When we sincerely took such a position, all sorts of remarkable things followed. We had a new Employer. Being all powerful, He provided what we needed, if we kept close to Him and performed His work well.

The book even offers a prayer to go with that step. I use the prayer often, especially when dealing with work. Here are a few lines that guide me often: "God, I offer myself to Thee, to build with me and to do with me as Thou wilt. Relieve me of the bondage of self, that I may better do Thy will."

Once I surrender, I have nothing to fear. With this new way of seeing it, I always have the same Boss, a God who loves me and wants the best for me.

Every day, I consult God for my assignment, my marching orders, my perfect good. The clarity doesn't come down like a hammer or a hurricane. It comes to me, not through any earthly boss, but from that most important Boss of all, the still, small voice within. For me, that voice is God. For others, it's that inner clarity and peace that comes from knowing, accepting, and loving who you truly are and honoring it above all other voices first, last, and always.

Power is an inside job.

The speaker onstage didn't care if anyone saw her sweat.

She wiped her brow but promised she wasn't having a hot flash.

"This is a power surge!" she bellowed.

We all felt the energy at the Spirit of Women in Business conference at Kent State University. More than 300 women attended the daylong conference about how to harness your power. First we heard from DeLores Pressley, a motivational speaker and coach who urges women to be "undeniably powerful."

"Women take care; men take charge," she said. "Men are taught to apologize for their weaknesses; women are taught to apologize for their strengths."

How true. I remember sitting with a group of fellow writers at a national conference of columnists when the man next to me asked what my plans for the future were. He was about ten years older and had been writing a column a few years longer. I told him I hoped to have a syndicated column one day, give inspirational talks, and write books.

"That's awful ambitious," he scoffed, then turned away and started talking to the men at the table. From the tone of his voice, his words didn't sound at all like a compliment. It sounded like one of those "Who do you think you are to dream so big?" kind of messages. It left me feeling small.

I wish I could have sat up taller, held my head higher, and said, "Yes, I'm excited and grateful to be blessed with so much ambition and passion and enthusiasm to spread my message to anyone in the world who needs or wants it."

Unfortunately, I was too dumbfounded and shamed to make a quick comeback. If only I could have quoted Timothy Leary, who said, "Women who seek to be equal with men lack ambition." Or shared Marianne Williamson's words that everyone should commit to memory: "You are a child of God. Your playing small does not serve the world. There's nothing enlightened about shrinking so that other people won't feel insecure around you."

She's right. Your smallness doesn't make the world a grander place. My success benefits everyone and everyone else's success benefits me. It's not just our shadow selves and weaknesses we need to stop fearing. We all need to stop being afraid of our own light, stop being afraid of our power and what it might mean to tap into it, all the way down to the core of that nuclear reactor that is the indwelling Spirit of God most alive in us.

Yes, we were all born to glorify the God who lives and dwells in each of us. We're here to use up every bit of that power and energy and passion and light. When we shine, the world gets brighter for everyone, not just us.

People like DeLores remind us of that. She urged all of us to get a mentor and a coach. The more people on your side, the better. Get rid of the silent beliefs, those voices in your head that keep telling you, *You can't do it . . . You're a fraud . . . You're going to fail.*

Toss fear overboard. "When fear knocks on your door, don't give it the key," she said.

I needed to change my locks.

We heard from other great speakers at the conference. Barbara Blake, from Longview Associates and Sherpa Coaching, taught us how to coach ourselves. Leadership is a state of mind, not a job title. See yourself as a leader even if no one else does.

You always hear people say, "Get out of your comfort zone." Barbara said, "Grow your comfort zone." That sounds more inviting and less scary.

She told us to ask ourselves, *What should I stop doing?* "The power is in the stopping," she said. I used to think it was in starting more projects and plans. For starters, we could stop whining, complaining, and doubting. Stop interrupting others, talking over people, and being afraid of success.

Barbara urged us all to stop using the f word.

No, not that one.

The female f word: *feel.*

Don't tell your board of directors, "I feel like we should

invest more." Don't tell your client, "I feel we can increase sales." Don't tell your employees, "I feel we will succeed." Don't tell your boss, "I feel like we're doing the best we can."

Cut the f word out and make your point forcefully: "We should...we can...we will...we are."

Then Leslie Ungar, president of Electric Impulse Communications, told us how to develop the diva within. I never before had anyone give me permission to be a diva. It felt wildly exciting.

Diva is Italian for "female deity." It used to be reserved for the celebrated singer, the outstanding talent. I like the idea of celebrating your inner goddess and letting her out.

Find out what you need to feel empowered. We all need something, Leslie said. It could be shoulder pads, power ties, red lipstick, pearls, or a tattoo. She told the story of a man who remarked on her high heels. She told him she wore them to feel powerful. He said he didn't need anything to make him feel powerful.

She asked him what kind of car he drove.

"A BMW," he answered.

"That's what you need to feel powerful," she told him.

We laughed. A pair of Manolo Blahniks are soooo much cheaper.

What's it mean to be a diva? Whenever you get the chance to be onstage, own it. Own your real estate, your office, your cubicle, your workstation. Make people believe they can't do without you. Be confident enough to ask questions, to speak up, to ask for what you need to be your best self at work and beyond. Know your brand and communicate it. Stand out.

Whenever you are in the spotlight, shine bright. That doesn't mean just focusing on you, but rather focusing on how others are better off having heard or met you.

And if they see you sweat, they'll know it's because of your power, not your fear.

It's up to you to launch your life.

My favorite greeting card shows a biplane in the air with this quote above it:

Orville Wright didn't have a pilot's license.

Open the card and it reads, *Go change the world.*

That's what the Wright brothers did. They changed everyone's world when their plane left the ground. They were the first real pilots breaking new ground—the air.

I think about that every time I look at my vision board. There's a picture of their plane on it.

I believe we all can fly. Why? I'm from Ohio.

We're not just first in flight; Ohio is first, second, and third. It's the birthplace of aviation. Orville and Wilbur Wright built airplanes in Dayton. Ohio gave birth to John Glenn, the first American to orbit the earth. Then the Buckeye State produced Neil Armstrong, the first human to walk on the moon.

In my home state, we put the possible in impossible.

In eighth grade, I had the honor to meet John Glenn. Back then, that freckle-faced astronaut was the biggest hero around. In Ohio history, we learned about those restless brothers who opened a bicycle shop in Dayton. Orville and Wilbur didn't just build bicycles. They built gliders and kites, motors and propellers. They built the first wind tunnel, to test the wing surface of the airplanes they invented.

After the historic flight at Kitty Hawk, they returned to Ohio to perfect the plane, which led to the creation of the first dependable airplane. Their original airplane bears this inscription at the Smithsonian Institution:

The world's first power-driven, heavier-than-air machine in which man made free, controlled, and sustained flight. Invented and built by Wilbur and Orville Wright. Flown by them at Kitty Hawk, North Carolina[,] December 17, 1903. By original scientific research the Wright Brothers discovered the principles of human flight. As inventors, builders, and flyers they further developed the aeroplane, taught man to fly, and opened the era of aviation.

They opened the door for Neil Armstrong, who got his pilot's license at 15, before he learned to drive. He was born in Wapakoneta, Ohio, population 9,843. The quiet, humble man was an engineer and a Navy fighter pilot who flew 78 combat missions in the Korean War. He was in college when someone else broke the sound barrier. He was disappointed to miss out on what he thought was the greatest adventure in flight. Little did he know what was ahead of him.

In 1969, he took us all to the moon with him on Apollo 11. I'll never forget those words when he landed the lunar craft: "Houston, Tranquility Base here. The Eagle has landed." Or when he took that first step and said, "That's one small step for man, one giant leap for mankind." On that flight, he carried with him a piece of the original plane the Wright brothers flew.

Armstrong was a reluctant hero who hid from the media spotlight and rarely talked to reporters. He became a professor, bought a farm in Ohio, and disappeared back into his life. He knew he had completed his mission in life.

How do you know what yours is?

I once saw a poster at church and knew instantly it was my job assignment for life: *Inspire the world. Live your vocation.*

Inspire the world. That was it.

I keep a tiny plaque on my desk that bears this definition of inspire: *To affect, guide, or arouse by divine influence. To fill with enlivening or exalting emotion. To stimulate action; motivate. To affect or touch.*

Underneath it is my personal mission statement: *To inspire men and women to find and use their Inner Power, to find and complete their Sacred Mission, to create a greater life for themselves and others.*

If the word *mission* scares you away, call it something else. Søren Kierkegaard described it this way: "God has given each of us our 'marching orders.' Our purpose here on earth is to find those orders and carry them out."

I heard the call to carry them out near Kitty Hawk where the first flight took place on a remote stretch of sand.

Almost every year we vacation in the Outer Banks of North

Carolina, but I never visited the memorial until my friend Beth joined us back in 2007. I barely knew her, but my husband knew her husband and invited them to join us for a week on the beach. As soon as she arrived and we saw each other's inspirational books we had brought along, we knew we were soul mates.

At the end of a wonderful week together sharing our deepest dreams, we went to the Wright Brothers Memorial to launch our new life. We joked that we were the Right Sisters. We walked up to the official memorial, a 60-foot monument, and the words blew me away: "Dauntless Resolution. Unconquerable Faith." Those were the qualities the brothers had. Those were the qualities I wanted.

There are four stone markers to commemorate the four flights made on December 17, 1903. The first flight traveled just 120 feet; the second made it 175 feet; the third made it 200 feet. The last attempt was the best. The plane flew 852 feet.

A wonderful breeze blew through me as I stood on the flight path that first plane had taken. I walked from the starting point, the liftoff point, to the first marker where the first flight ended. There, I gave thanks for the first part of my life's journey that I had taken as a single parent with Gabrielle. That unplanned pregnancy, which once seemed like such a big mistake, had been the greatest gift of my life.

As I walked to the second marker, I gave thanks for the journey I had taken with friends in recovery who helped heal my childhood wounds. On my way to the third marker, I offered thanks for the journey I had taken with my husband. His undying love and loyalty saw me through cancer. He also helped launch my career as a columnist. He believed in me before I could.

I stood at the third stone and looked far down at the last stone. It was time to really and truly embrace my writing. There at Kitty Hawk, where man first took flight, I let go of my fear of success and my fear of failure. I was afraid to release being a journalist to become an author, that earliest of all my dreams. I had been afraid to let go of who I had been to fully embrace who I could be.

I stood at the third stone with the breeze as my only companion. It was time to say yes. Yes to all the writing that was in me to release. I felt the Spirit move through me. I opened my heart and offered all of me to God. I launched my dream life: to write all the books in me, to tell all my stories, to share everything life taught me to inspire others. I held my arms out like wings, and I swear the Holy Spirit supplied the lift and carried me to that final marker. I felt a new freedom and a new happiness.

I once read that there's the thing you do for a living and then there's the thing you were born to do. I was finally ready to do the thing I was born to do.

Once home, I taped the brochure from the Wright Memorial with the black-and-white photo of that plane on my vision board. I made the covers to all the books I wanted to write and posted them there. Then I wrote at the top: *This or something better.*

Was it okay to tell God what I wanted? Should I seek my heart's desire or God's will? Then I remembered what Beth told me: God's will is your heart's purest desire. They are one and the same.

Was it okay to post it there in the open? I knew it was when Beth sent me this quote from Habakkuk, a chapter of the Bible that I had never even heard of:

Then the Lord answered me and said: Write down the vision clearly upon the tablets, so that one can read it readily. For the vision still has its time, presses on to fulfillment, and will not disappoint. If it delays, wait for it, it will surely come, it will not be late.

Wait and it will surely come.
God is rarely early, but God is never late.

Things don't happen to you; they happen for
you and for others.

One of the hardest parts of getting cancer is losing your hair to chemotherapy.

When you're bald from chemo, you feel powerless. To the world, you're a patient. People stare. Friends cringe. Children flee.

When I had breast cancer 16 years ago, I planned to go right from my hair to a wig that looked just like me. No one would know I was bald from chemo. My husband took me shopping. We went looking for a wig while I was still under the influence of the cancer diagnosis. It wasn't pretty. Wig stores should carry a warning: Do Not Shop Until the Shock Has Worn Off. I felt paralyzed by anger, grief, and fear. I ended up outside the store sitting on the steps crying.

I was scared and sad and had no idea how to buy a hairpiece. We spent $500 on a human hair wig. The owner of a fancy salon guaranteed he would make it look just like my real hair. He even took a photo of me to guide the styling of the wig. He held my hand and promised it would be ready before my hair started to fall out.

Instead, he ruined the wig.

When my hair started falling out, he wouldn't return my phone calls. When the salon owner finally agreed to meet with us, he showed me the damaged wig and blamed me for bringing him an "inferior" wig. No apology, no refund. He charged me $190 for "styling" it. I was too weak from chemo to argue.

The wig was so overpermed, it looked like roadkill. I wore it for a whole two hours. It looked like hell, felt like hell, and reminded me of the hell that creep put us through. I threw it in the closet and never wore it again. It has become a Halloween costume.

The man left us no time to buy another one. Patches of hair were falling out. I looked like a dog with mange. My husband, my prince, helped me shave my head the day I was eating breakfast and saw bangs in my Cheerios. I ended up walking around bald for six months.

I can laugh about it now, but, boy, did I cry back then. Rivers.

No other woman should go through that, I vowed.

But I didn't do anything about it. What should I do? Report him to the Better Business Bureau? Sue him in small-claims court? I was so focused on the problem, it never occurred to me to be part of the solution for other cancer survivors.

Years passed. One day I went to Fort Wayne, Indiana, to speak at a cancer tribute dinner for Cancer Services of Northeast Indiana. I walked into their agency and nearly fell over. They had an entire wig salon with more than 150 beautiful wigs on display, organized by hair color. When I found out the wigs were free for the borrowing, I cried.

Women bald from cancer treatment can check out two wigs at a time, like you would books from a library. When they're returned, the wigs go straight to the salon, where volunteers shampoo and style them for the next woman.

The room felt warm and inviting, like a real beauty salon.

Then I heard about Debra Brown and knew I had to act. She came to the Fort Wayne agency one day to find a wig, but there were only two wigs for African American women. She didn't like either one. She already felt depressed and discouraged from cancer treatments and losing her hair. The lack of diversity at the salon made her angry—angry enough to do something. She called her family, her friends, and every church that would listen. She got the Fort Wayne Urban League involved. She asked them all to donate money or wigs. Her goal? One hundred wigs. She didn't want any other African American woman walking out of that salon disappointed.

In three months, Debra had 200 wigs to donate. She told everyone, "It's not about me. God put it on my heart."

That's when it hit me to create a place where women who are experiencing hair loss from cancer treatments can get free wigs. The Gathering Place, which offers free help to anyone touched by cancer, got on board.

As soon as I shared my idea, they started creating a salon at their Beachwood location. They made a cozy, private space with a big mirror and bright lights and lots of shelves for all the wigs we were going to collect.

I wrote a column that we needed wigs. Wigs for brunettes, blondes, and redheads. Wigs for women with gray hair. Wigs for women of all races. Wigs of all shapes, colors, and styles. Wigs of synthetic hair, since human hair is harder to maintain.

I asked people to get their church, school, or family to donate new and "pre-loved" wigs to the Gathering Place. We needed money to buy new wigs and wig hair products. We also needed beauticians willing to donate time to clean and style wigs.

We decided to send a message to every woman touched by cancer: losing hair doesn't mean losing hope. We wanted to give them peace of mind. We called the salon HairPeace.

Within weeks, more than 500 wigs were donated to the Gathering Place, along with more than $38,000. People all over Greater Cleveland wanted in. Philanthropist Sam Miller donated $3,000. "I'm in for a couple hundred wigs," he said. "I know what this disease does to people." He's been fighting cancer for more than ten years.

Students at the Academy of Saint Bartholomew in Middleburg Heights collected more than $700. In one kindergarten classroom, children got to pin hair on wig heads when they donated money. On Saint Patrick's Day, students donated a dollar to "dress down" for the day. The Knitting Angels of Bainbridge, from the Church of the Holy Angels, donated wigs. A visiting nurses agency sponsored a drive to collect "pre-loved" wigs.

Dozens called in tears and offered to donate the wigs of their wives, mothers, and sisters who had died from cancer. The response was so big, the Gathering Place opened another wig salon in its center on the west side of Cleveland.

Before we were open for business, an older woman came to the Gathering Place for a massage wearing a baseball hat over a long gray wig. When she saw the wigs, she asked if the staff could set one aside for her until HairPeace opened. Eileen Coan, the medical librarian, didn't want her to wait. Eileen loves to tell the story:

"We closed the door, she took off her wig, and she pointed hesitantly to a short curly one and whispered, 'I always wanted *curly* hair.' She put it on, had an ear-to-ear grin and the beginning of tears. She whispered, 'I *love* it.' I started to put her old wig in the bag. 'Oh no,' she stated confidently. 'That one stays here; this is all I need!'"

Another young woman, who was thin from chemotherapy, came in to meet with a nutritionist. Her short, perky wig looked good but was too big. Every time she sneezed she feared it would pop off. Eileen described her joy in this e-mail:

I got her set up with a cap liner and told her to take her time looking. She chose a more sophisticated straight look with some subtle highlights. One look in the mirror and she clapped. "THIS is the one I want!" She stepped out into the library and told the room full of eight strangers, "Look at my new hair," and they all clapped, too. She told us to give her old one to someone else, and she headed out to show her mom her new look.

A couple came in together, eyes red from crying. They had been to wig stores and were ready to give up. The wife's hair was scheduled to fall out within days. Every wig they tried had too much hair until the woman spied a little pixie blond wig. It fit just right. Her husband smiled. They left holding hands.

Another woman came in with her husband. She was newly bald and reluctant to enter. Then she spotted a wig that looked like her original hair. She tried it on, loved it, and asked her husband to come in. He stood silently at the door, then said, "My beautiful bride is back."

One woman who had just found out she would need chemo stopped by. She wanted a wig that was thin and wispy like her hair. Sure enough, she found one. She tried it on then told the staff, "I'll come back when I need it and hope that it is still here." They handed her the wig.

"It can't be that easy," the woman said.

Yes, it can.

To donate for wigs, send a check to: The Gathering Place, 23300 Commerce Park, Cleveland, Ohio 44122. Or visit www.touchedby cancer.org.

Don't die with your music in you.

Rocco Scotti is Cleveland's own Yankee Doodle Dandy.

He has sung the national anthem probably more times than anyone in the world. He sang it at nearly every Indians game for 20 years.

He sang it at a home opener an hour after he left a hospital with stitches from a car wreck that knocked him unconscious. He sang it for Presidents Gerald Ford and Ronald Reagan. He sang it at six public venues in one day. He sang it at stadiums in New York, Pittsburgh, and Baltimore; at the Football Hall of Fame in Canton; and at the Baseball Hall of Fame in Cooperstown, New York.

Rocco sang it for nearly every major league baseball team. He sang it at football games. He sang it nearly 50 times a year for 20 years.

He sang it so well, he received a Civilian Purple Heart for

"inspiring patriotism through his exceptional performing of 'The Star-Spangled Banner.'"

He believes God called him to make the national anthem his one-hit wonder. It wasn't what he set out to do.

Rocco was born in 1920 in Ambler, Pennsylvania, grew up in a family of 14 children, and moved to Cleveland when he was three. Like most kids back then, he dreamed of becoming a baseball player. He followed his dad into the construction business instead, carrying 100-pound bags on his shoulders. His dad sang around the house, so Rocco started singing, too. He worked with a voice coach. He met his wife, June, in 1945, and they moved to New York where he could study opera.

Rocco's career as an opera singer never took off, so he moved to Los Angeles and studied with a tenor. He sang pop tunes in nightclubs for a while. His singing career stalled, so he moved back to Cleveland. He worked construction, took voice classes, and sang the national anthem at random events. Back then, he sang it straight up, the same way everyone else did.

Then one day he decided to dress it up, to add something unique.

He was asked to sing the anthem for a Cleveland Indians–Baltimore Orioles game. As he was driving to the game, Rocco wondered what he could do to make it different. He added a high G at the end. He's not sure Francis Scott Key would approve, but the guys in both dugouts loved it when Rocco first tried it two decades ago.

When he gets to "the land of the free, and the home of the brave." He hangs on to the word *free* and the last *the* for as long as he can. No one had heard it sung that way. Everyone loved it. From then on, he was asked to sing it at every game.

His favorite time? He had just finished the song when he was told someone in the stands wanted to meet him. It was baseball Hall of Famer Earl Averill, a six-time All-Star and Rocco's idol. Rocco was so overcome, he sat next to Earl and cried.

That and singing for the presidents were the best times.

"They seemed to like it," Rocco said.

He hates that so many singers botch the national anthem. "Almost nobody does it well," he said. It's a hard song. Too many people try to wing it, and they start with a broken wing.

Roseanne Barr screeched it. Michael Bolton forgot it. Steven Tyler changed it. (At a racetrack in 2001, he closed the anthem by singing "and the home of the Indianapolis 500.") But those weren't the worst versions. "Robert Goulet," Rocco said, shaking his head. "He was too drunk to finish it."

"Do it well or don't do it at all. It means something," Rocco said.

Some performers sing the national anthem for an ego trip, to get in front of a crowd on TV, Rocco said. "They don't care enough about it. You have to treat it with respect." He always did. Before the words left his lips, a prayer did.

And you have to practice. Rocco used to practice in his car until the day he hit a high note and cracked his side window. In three places. From then on, he practiced with the windows down.

He has sung other anthems, too. The Polish national anthem for boxing team matches. He sang the Hungarian national anthem for basketball games, the Italian national anthem for soccer games, and the Israeli national anthem when the assistant prime minister of Israel was in Cleveland.

But he never tired of the old "Star-Spangled Banner." Every time, he felt a connection to his country. "It's a challenge every time to do it well," he said.

Rocco and his bride, June, have been married for more than 60 years. He was 89 when we talked. By then, he had been retired from the majors. When the Cleveland Indians started playing at their new stadium, the team brought in new voices. Rocco is a good sport about it.

"Things change. Life goes on," he tells people. "Everything comes to an end."

He has no regrets, no hard feelings. But if they called, would he sing it for them?

Rocco grinned and said, "I'd ask, 'What time?'"

Every so often there is talk of changing the anthem from "The Star-Spangled Banner" to "America the Beautiful" or "God Bless America." Reporters call Rocco and ask his opinion.

"They're pretty songs, but they don't have the built-in drama of 'The Star Spangled Banner.' It has character. It creates patriotism. It demands such attention," he said.

He loves "The Star-Spangled Banner." "The rockets' red glare, the bombs bursting in air" aren't just words to him. They're family history. His brother Nicholas died in World War II. Nick was a sergeant in the infantry. He was only 19.

Rocco was 24 when his brother died. It hit him hard. When Nick went into the service, he told Rocco, "I'm not coming back." Rocco shared a verse from a poem he wrote about Nick: "Now there are white crosses lying one next to each other; every night I say a prayer for them, for among them is my brother."

The difference between the way Rocco sings the national anthem and the way everyone else does is this: every time Rocco belts out those final words, "O, say does that star-spangled banner yet wave, O'er the land of the free, and the home of the brave?" he knows the answer is yes.

Rocco grew quiet when he talked about how that song turned into his gift to share with the world. "It's strange, but something happened that made it that way," he said. "It's like someone said, 'This is gonna be your thing.'"

And once you find your thing, you treat it with respect.

"Work very sincerely with it," Rocco urged. "Make it really mean something to you and those who will hear it."

His life story is a great reminder that we all have music in us, even those of us who can't sing a note. I used to attend a church where the music director urged everyone to sing, even those who weren't sure they had it in them. "If you sing off-key," he'd always say, "then sing even louder."

We all have a song to sing. A song that someone out there needs to hear, just the way it comes from our hearts and our lips.

Nothing you want is upstream, so stop struggling.

Got a crisis? Call my husband.

That's his specialty.

Not only does he talk me down from the ledge of whatever small speed bump I'm dangling from, certain I'm on the verge of a catastrophe, but, as I mentioned earlier, he co-owns a crisis communications firm called Hennes Paynter Communications. They have made it their specialty to help people and companies all over the country respond during a crisis.

When people hear what he does for a living, they often think he helps companies and executives spin their way out of trouble. Not at all. Bruce tells everyone you can't spin your way out of bad behavior. His mantra is "Tell the truth, tell it all, tell it first."

There's never a shortage of companies in crisis, so business is good. A few years ago, a man approached Bruce and his business partner about a job. They made the decision not to hire him. Months later, the man was hired by a competitor who owned a much larger full-service PR firm that wanted to go head-to-head with them. Then Bruce read in the newspaper that the firm had hired two others to create a crisis communications unit to compete with Bruce.

At first my husband was worried. What would it mean to have competition? How much business would this new venture take from them? Would there be enough business for both companies to succeed? Would they have to struggle neck and neck to compete for clients?

Then he did something that made me admire him even more than I already did. He relaxed. He made a decision not to give in to fear, not to believe in scarcity or competition or the idea that you have to constantly struggle to get ahead in life and in business. He decided to keep doing what he did and keep doing it better. Then he wrote the owner of the business an e-mail congratulating him on starting the new business venture and wished him great success. Bruce even wrote that there was surely enough work for everyone. Then he went over the top and said, "If I'm ever in a position to send you business, I will."

The man was stunned when he received such a gracious note from the person others might see as his biggest competitor. The man called my husband and left a message on voice mail expressing his deep gratitude. The man's voice broke as he told Bruce what that e-mail meant to him.

Bruce taught me that we don't have to struggle to attract more of what we want. There is no competition, no scarcity.

What about the global competition? What about the person in the other cubicle competing? Not your concern.

A friend once gave me a CD by Esther Hicks. These five words changed my life: *Nothing you want is upstream.*

I burst out laughing when I heard her say that. So often I find myself fighting against the current, working against all odds to get to someplace I think will make me happier than where the flow of life gently invites me to go. I waste a lot of energy and time before exhaustion forces me to surrender and float to the place life has prepared for me alone. Once you stop struggling against the current—because it is always going to win—you can align yourself with what is, rest, and allow the river of life to carry you along to the place where you can make the biggest difference with your life.

The Bible constantly reminds us to let go and let God handle whatever it is we're trying to control. As the Gospel of Matthew says, the lilies of the field don't labor or spin:

> If that is how God clothes the grass of the field, which is here today and tomorrow is thrown into the fire, will he not much more clothe you—you of little faith? So do not worry, saying, "What shall we eat?" or "What shall we drink?" or "What shall we wear?"...Your heavenly Father knows that you need them. But seek first his kingdom and his righteousness, and all these things will be given to you as well. Therefore do not worry about tomorrow, for tomorrow will worry about itself.

All that worrying and extra work doesn't buy you a smidge of serenity, according to Psalm 127: "In vain is your earlier rising, your going later to rest. You who toil for the bread you eat, when he pours gifts on his beloved while they sleep."

For years I was baffled by the saying "Take the path of least resistance." It's hard to see which path that is when you're resisting them all out of fear. Then I finally got it: stop resisting. As they used to say on *Star Trek: The Next Generation*: "Resistance is futile." It really is. God does the real work, we don't. All we have to do is simply cooperate with grace, without struggle or strain. My old way was to suffer, try, work, agonize, worry, sweat, and struggle. My new way? Release, allow, surrender, trust, believe, and relax. The shortcut is God.

You don't have to try so hard to be great. One day I was all in a tizzy over which column to write. My problem normally isn't coming up with an idea, it's that I come up with too many and struggle over which one to choose. I had asked God for clarity and got it when my daughter called and said, "Do what is easy."

I wrote that on a sticky note that smiles at me every day. God does the heavy lifting. I'm always awed when I see the work of Michelangelo, who simply released the figures from the marble. All I need to do is move my fingers and release the words that God gives me. That doesn't mean everything comes easy to me, but writing comes out of me when I let it.

What's easy for one person isn't what comes easy for others. Math comes easy for others. Not me. I have the proof. My college ACT scores. I got a 17 in math. Back then, the high was 28. At first I was ashamed of it. Now it's a reminder to stick with what comes easy, and math isn't it. Writing is easy when I just try to write like Regina Brett. It gets complicated and messy when I try to write like someone who I think is better than me.

My friend Barb used to tell me there is no competition. When you lie out in the sun to get a tan, you aren't competing with anyone for the rays. There is enough sun for all. God's love and direction is enough for each of us and for all of us.

I remembered her words when I first became a newspaper columnist. The good news was that the editor gave me a column. The bad news was, he also gave three other people in the same newsroom a column. Would there be enough ideas to go around? I've been writing columns for 19 years and have yet to run out of ideas. The goal isn't to be better than the other writers. The goal is to be better than the last column I wrote. Success is never about undercutting others to get to the top. The top of what?

There was a brief period when I suffered from terrible envy of another writer. I envied her talent and awards and success, even though I had my own. How could I get her off my radar screen? Instead of booting her off, I made her my prayer partner. Every time I thought of her or heard her name or read about her success, I saw it as a call from her soul to mine to pray for her. So I kept throwing Hail Marys at her. She became even more successful, which drove me crazy until I realized her success was blessing the world, and so was mine. The world needed us both.

There's room for all of us in our own particular spot. My divine assignment has my name on it, no one else's. So does yours. When you live the life you alone were created to live, there is no competition. There's enough for everyone and no reason to struggle.

Create a pocket of greatness right where you are.

Y ou want to change the world?

Change the workplace and you change the world.

People spend nearly a third of their lives working. Every boss and business owner, large and small, can have a huge impact on that third. You can change the world one employee at a time. One customer at a time. One client at a time. One patient at a time. One coworker at a time. When you change their world, you change the world for their children, spouses, and pets.

How?

When people have a bad day at work, they go home and take it out on their spouses, who take it out on the children, who take it out on the dog. When people have a great day, they send out ripples of joy.

Imagine if each boss took a good, hard look at what they

paid their staff. On paper, those things look like simple benefits that cost the company. But in real life, they're so much more. A salary increase means someone can afford to buy a house instead of renting an apartment. It means the difference between a car that breaks down and a car that can get a family all the way to Grandma's house for Thanksgiving.

What a person is paid determines what's under the tree at Christmas, whether a child gets to play in the band at school. I remember in eighth grade when I wanted to play the flute. My dad went with me to the band meeting. He shook his head and told me, "You'll pass out." He didn't tell me the truth: we couldn't afford it.

Employers have a lot of power, like the power to provide funeral leave. When my dad died, no workplace kept my five brothers and five sisters from traveling in from Arizona, New York, Indiana, Florida, and Michigan to be in that front row at Immaculate Conception Church to hold up my mom as she let go of my dad.

The power to provide personal days means you can take the day off to be with your mother on her birthday, the first one she spends alone after your dad died. Maternity and paternity leaves mean new parents can bond with a baby. Vacation time means a family can create memories for a lifetime.

Sick leave, what a gift. When I had cancer in 1998, I had to worry about losing my hair and losing my lunch to chemotherapy, but I never had to worry about losing my job if I took too much time off. I didn't need to skimp on the daily radiation treatments, because my company offered good insurance coverage.

Dental insurance will determine whether a child with

crooked teeth turns into an adult who can smile. The braces the company insurance provides show up in all those family pictures in every album. That smile? Imagine being the boss who provided it.

Some companies offer insurance that covers fertility. How powerful to make it possible to turn a couple into parents for life.

Flexible hours and scheduling mean a mom can get off work in time to see her son hit a home run. It means a daughter will know that her dad saw her kick the winning goal in soccer. Companies worry about the global marketplace but shouldn't lose sight of the importance of the backyard catch with Dad.

And finally, there's retirement. Because of good benefits, seniors won't have to cut their high blood pressure pills in half or be shamed into asking their children if they can move in.

All because of the risks a boss takes, the choices an employer makes. It's not about creating jobs or even creating great jobs, it's about creating great workplaces so employees can create a great world.

Employers have incredible power over people's lives. Two of the most powerful words in the English language are *You're hired*. Remember how powerful those words were to you? Remember the day that call came and you heard those words? You called your spouse, your kids, your parents. Or these words: *You got a raise*. The relief. The celebration. The pride. The gratitude. The bills you could finally pay.

It's amazing what companies can do to make work a joy for others. I once gave a keynote address at the NorthCoast 99 honoring the 99 best places to work in Northeast Ohio. The program was developed by the Employers Resource Council, which is dedicated to fostering the best HR practices, programs, and services. I was amazed at all the things companies did to celebrate and honor their workers. Some places offered aerobics classes, a yoga room, fitness centers, or gym memberships. Others provided on-site day-care centers and tuition reimbursement. I love that Hyland Software offers surprise visits from the ice cream truck. The eight-month-old daughter of an employee of one company got a piece of plastic stuck in her throat and couldn't breathe. Her mom saved her life because she had learned the Heimlich maneuver at work.

At ADP in Independence, Ohio, employees visit the elderly with Alzheimer's and those in hospice care. They adopt seniors, serve meals, and collect for school supplies for children. At Weaver Leather in Mount Hope, one year each employee adopted a foster child for Valentine's Day and stuffed duffel bags with items from a wish list. For some children, that bag was the only personal item they owned.

MCPc Inc., a Strongsville IT company, holds chili cook-offs, Hawaiian shirt day, Easter egg hunts, and car washes where the bosses wash the cars.

It was fascinating to hear that some companies provide dry cleaning and laundry service, an on-site hair salon and barber, access to a doctor or nurse at work, and free mammograms. Others offer free oil changes, travel agents, and tax preparation.

I left the event hoping more employers might be creative and give people a paid month off every five years, an all-expense-paid vacation every 20 years, discounts on computers or cell phone service, or share access to company discounts at hotels, restaurants, and amusement parks.

Even at small businesses, it doesn't take a lot of money to fill a candy jar or provide doughnuts to make a boring meeting go a little faster. It won't break the bank to let employees leave a few hours early on Friday, or to stock a refrigerator with fresh fruit or create a coffee bar with free coffee, tea, and hot chocolate.

The best employers make it possible for people to make a living and a life, and better yet, a difference. By changing the workplace, they change the lives of all those around them, which means they're changing the world.

Even when you feel invisible, your work isn't.

It's easy for some people to feel invisible at work.

Every time we went for a drive in my small town, my dad used to point out every roof he'd repaired or replaced. He had a story to tell about every house we passed in Ravenna, Ohio. He would tell us who lived there, who they were related to, how many children they had, and what they all did for a living. The people who lived in those homes probably forgot who climbed that ladder, carried that spouting, and hammered those shingles under a burning sun, but my dad never did.

Turns out they didn't either. When he died at 83, the funeral home was full of people grateful for the roofs over their heads and the man who put them there.

The world is full of people whose work matters long after they've touched it. Some of those people were at my dad's funeral, like our mail carrier, Tony. He was steady as clockwork on Sycamore Street, showing up at 10 a.m. every day. He cushioned the blow of the gas bill with a grin and a story about his latest win at the bowling alley.

Those people are everywhere in our lives. People like Doctor Neely, the family physician who still made house calls and rarely ever sent a bill to my parents. People like my appliance repairman, Sruly Wolf, who comes at a moment's notice when the rinse cycle stops on the washer or the dryer quits when it's full of wet clothes. He trims a few bucks off the bill and sends us a turkey and a basket of food every Thanksgiving to thank us for being faithful customers.

In his other life, he's a humble rabbi and a police chaplain in Cleveland, Ohio. He once received an award for saving the life of an unconscious off-duty police officer. Sruly, who was in Chicago on business, was walking down a street and saw the officer in a smoke-filled car and pulled the unconscious man free. When a reporter interviewed him, he downplayed it, saying, "Look, I just went to Chicago that week to attend a trade show."

Everyone leaves a mark. It's up to each of us how we leave it and where. When my husband and I had our fireplace tile replaced, the man who did the work spent long hours trying to get the fireproofing wall in place to protect us. Our home was built in 1920 and the brick was nearly 100 years old. It gave him major headaches, breaking every nail he drilled into it. When he finally got it right, I asked him to sign the fireboard. He smiled as he scribbled his name, Donovan, on that wall in marker. No one would ever see it once the tile went up, but it truly was a work of art and I wanted him to know it.

We tend to measure our worth by the big highlights that mean the most to us, not the small moments that mean the most to others. I had the privilege to hear about one of those moments from a man who spent 28 years as a firefighter.

There were calls that made Tom Schultz cry, calls that made him laugh, and calls that made him fear for his life.

One time a tired new mother fell asleep on her couch with her one-month-old baby. "One woke up and one didn't," Tom said softly.

Another time, an old woman stopped answering her phone and picking up deliveries. Neighbors called her, but no one answered. They called her son in Toledo. Her son called her, but no one answered, so he called 911. The firefighters banged on her windows. No answer. They looked in the window and didn't see anyone. Their supervisor told them to break down the door.

When they did, they saw the old woman sitting in a chair with the phone next to her. They said, "Ma'am, the neighbors called and your son called; why didn't you answer?" She looked up and said, "It's my phone and I'll answer it if I want to."

Then there was the woman who fled after the sausage she had left burning on the stove caught the house on fire. She got her children out and slammed the door behind her. That cut off the flames but left the fire smoldering.

A fire can double in size every minute. When Tom opened the door, black smoke poured out. Tom was at the tip of the hose, the first one in, with the next firefighter six feet behind him on the hose. He couldn't see him, but he could hear him. They walked through the pitch-black house. The air from opening the door reignited the fire. The third firefighter coming in mistakenly yanked on the hose. It flew out of Tom's hands.

Oh no, he thought. The hose is your lifeline out. You can't see a door. The hose is the only way to find your way back out.

It was the longest ten seconds of Tom's life. He thought about the wife and kids he'd never see again. Then he heard the voice of the firefighter behind him: "I still have the hose." They got out safely.

No one touched him more deeply than the old lady with the plums.

He tried to share the story with the firefighters at his retirement breakfast, but the words couldn't get past the lump in his throat. He cried as he told it to me.

Early in his career he got a 911 call one summer: *lady down in backyard*. The woman was in her 90s and had fallen off a stepladder near a plum tree. It was late summer and all the plums were ripe. She had a compound fracture of her ankle. The neighbors had called for help. Tom helped dress and splint the wound, then transport her to the hospital.

A doctor said she would need surgery to fix the break. She would have to spend the night. Tom didn't remember her name, but all day long she was on his mind. He never imagined she'd stay with him the rest of his career.

He wondered, *Why would an elderly lady with all her wits put herself in danger on a ladder to pick plums?* The next morning when his shift ended, he drove back to her house, still in uniform, and picked her a bag of plums. He took them to the hospital.

When he found her room, he introduced himself and

handed her the plums. She was quiet for a minute, then told him why those plums were so important to her.

She said she had no family. She had outlived everyone. She was picking the plums to make plum jelly to thank all the neighbors who looked out for her, who were her family.

She thanked Tom for the plums. "I made her day, but she made my career," Tom said. "I'm just an average guy. She showed me I could make a difference in people's lives."

Before being a firefighter, Tom had worked a job he hated at a machine shop, where he felt like a machine. He loved the outdoors and hated punching a time clock and working inside all day for ten hours.

Tom was the oldest rookie when he started as a firefighter on May 7, 1984, at age 35. He retired at 63. He planned to tell the plum story at his farewell breakfast but got too emotional to finish. He wanted to leave behind more than his picture hanging on the wall of the fire station. He wanted to leave the rookies with that plum story.

He wanted them to remember to treat everyone with the utmost respect, dignity, and compassion at every emergency.

He wanted them to know the thing that mattered most in life was simply to make a difference in someone else's life.

You make a living by what you get;
you make a life by what you give.

Want to be rich?

Share what's in your pocket. It's not your money anyway.

Sounds absurd, doesn't it?

That's what I used to think. Not anymore.

One of the richest men in the world became rich only after he gave away all his money. Millard Fuller was famous for saying, "I see life as both a gift and a responsibility. My responsibility is to use what God has given me to help His people in need."

He set a goal early on: get rich.

His marketing business made him a millionaire at 29. It also made him miserable. After his marriage and health suffered, he sold the cars and the boat and gave his money to the poor. Then he started building them houses all over the world. His wife, Linda, worked for free. Fuller's salary was $15,000.

"God's money is just in the pockets of people," Fuller used to say. "We've got to extract it."

When the founder of Habitat for Humanity International died at 74, God's money remained in the roofs, walls, and plumbing in the homes of 1.5 million people all over the world. I once heard someone say, "All God wants is for you to take good care of His children." Fuller did that. So did Laura Bickimer.

She lived a simple life, lived all her life in the same home she grew up in. When the retired math teacher died at 93, she left $2.1 million to Baldwin Wallace University in Berea, Ohio. She graduated from there in 1936 and had attended on a scholarship. She never forgot the power of someone else's generosity. Part of her gift will go toward scholarships.

Bickimer never earned more than $40,000 a year. Imagine living on that when you have $2 million in the bank. She saved it for others.

She once wrote, "I have discovered that one's life can be quite simple and unspectacular, yet full and worthwhile!"

Hers turned out to be a simple and spectacular life.

Small donations can make big changes in the world. My friend Kevin Conroy is a Catholic priest serving the poorest of the poor. I once wrote a column about how he left Cleveland to work in Cambodia with the Maryknoll missionaries. He helps the Little Sprouts, 270 children orphaned by parents who died of AIDS. The children are all HIV-positive. He sometimes travels to the garbage dumps where families forage for food and things to sell.

After reading about his work, readers sent him checks for $10, $20, $50. One person gave $1,000. All the donations went toward building ten classrooms in a two-story building. The public school dedication was held on International Children's Day.

"Originally, we were just going to build one story and pray that in the future we could find the money to finish the job," Kevin told me. "I used the $10,000 that I raised from your column to help build the school."

The school principal asked Kevin what names he wanted to put on the school. "I am thinking of something like 'Friends from Cleveland, Ohio, USA,'" Kevin said.

You don't have to give millions. It's about giving a genuine gift from the heart. Before I met my husband, Bruce was just 35, struggling financially and barely making ends meet, when he had a moment that changed his life. He had just opened up his own public relations business when he attended a fund-raising event for the Jewish Community Federation. The meeting was at the home of one of the largest property developers in the country. After the 30 guests had dinner, they went into a room where Sam Miller, one of the most generous philanthropists in Cleveland, gave a passionate speech about the importance of helping the Jewish community.

People were so moved, one man stood and said, "I want you to know our family gift this year will be 1.2 million dollars." My husband gasped. Another man stood up and said, "My gift this year to the Jewish Community Federation will be $750,000." My husband gulped. They were going around the room, and everyone was going to announce their gift. Bruce broke out in a sweat. There were some rich people in that room, but he wasn't one of them. Most of them were 20 years older than him and 20 years further down the road of financial success.

When it was his turn, Bruce stood up and said, "I'm the youngest person here and I just opened my own business. I'm in debt up to my eyeballs, having financed my business with credit cards. I'm clearly not in the same caliber in business with all of you, but how could I not be moved by your generosity? I don't know how I will do it, but I gave $100 last year—and this year I will double my donation."

He got a standing ovation. They slapped him on the back in wild congratulations. They knew that he had dug the deepest to make the biggest stretch. What he learned from their reaction was that what matters isn't the size of the gift, it's the quality of the gift.

Quantity is nice, too. Bruce once worked at a car dealership for Lee Seidman. Lee opened the Motorcars Group in 1958. One year he decided to take a gamble on an automobile franchise no one else wanted. People thought he was nuts. It was called Toyota. Lee became one of the nation's largest auto dealers. He made millions. Then he gave it all away.

He could have left a hefty estate to his children and made them all multimillionaires. He could have spent his retirement taking cruises around the world. Instead, he went to Harvard and learned how to give his money away.

He gave $17 million to the Cleveland Clinic to create an endowed chair in functional neurosurgery and to help pay for medical research and build the clinic's heart center. He gave $1 million to University Hospitals Rainbow Babies & Children's Hospital for pediatric cancer innovation. He gave $6 million to Hillcrest Hospital so they could expand. Then he outdid even himself. He gave $42 million to University Hospitals to build a cancer hospital. The Seidman Cancer Center is ten stories tall and has 120 beds. It is the only freestanding cancer hospital in Northeast Ohio.

When his wife, Jane, looks at the building, she thinks of her dad, who died of cancer at 56. He never got to see his own grandchildren. Their gift will allow countless grandparents to live to see their grandchildren grow up. The Seidmans are spending their autumn years encouraging others to give their money away while they're still alive to see and shape its impact. He loves watching his bank account balance fall as each hospital grows. He's never felt richer.

When you share what God puts in your pocket, you realize you're richer than you ever imagined. Giving away money actually ensures that you will get more of it. I believe there's always enough to go around. I tell myself every day: *My abundance benefits everyone and their abundance benefits me.* The more I earn, the more I can give away, and as soon as I give it away, more shows up.

Years ago when I was a single parent with no money, my friend's family lost nearly everything they owned in a house fire. I wrote her a check for $80. It was all I could donate back then. That $80 sounds meager now, but back then, when I had nothing, it was a lot. Weeks later, I received a check for $80 from the college I attended. They had made an error in my financial aid and sent me the balance.

Recently, I felt that tug of the spirit to be more generous. It's time to put more abundance in the world. So I wrote out some checks to charities and to my niece and two nephews in college. It felt good to give back into the world.

An hour later, my cousin called. "Congratulations! Your phone must be ringing off the hook!" she shouted.

"What are you talking about?" I asked, puzzled.

"Your book was on TV!" she screamed.

What in the world was she talking about? It turns out that while I was writing out checks from abundance, *Today* show host Hoda Kotb was holding up my first book, *God Never Blinks*, to her TV viewers and urging them to read it.

When I got off the phone with my cousin, I paused, shook my head, and said, "Wow, God, You are *so* good!" I didn't even know it then, but that 30-second gush from Hoda sent my book to No. 11 on Amazon. *God Never Blinks* was No. 3 in self-help books, No. 2 in religious books, and No. 1 in spiritual books. The book had come out three years earlier.

Then God did one better.

That same week I learned that my friend's husband was going to Paris for a book signing. I called to congratulate her. How exciting that they were going to Paris. She had taken care of him when he had cancer and heart surgery and deserved a big bonus from life. She said she wouldn't be joining him. They hadn't yet received any royalties from the book, and things were stretched thin at home.

How could I not share my abundance with one of my dearest friends? So I got off the phone and went online. I found out the cost of a trip to Paris and wrote her a check and popped it in the mail. It felt so good to send more abundance into the world.

She called two days later. First she thanked me a million ways to Sunday, and then she said, "I tore up your check." What?

She didn't need it. The same day my check arrived, so did his royalty check. She was going to Paris. All I ended up giving her was a ride to the airport, but what a joyful ride it was.

I swear it's like a chain of giving that takes off and doesn't stop.

The more you believe in abundance, the more it believes in you. When you share what God puts in your pocket, you're always richer than you thought.

Be somebody's hero.

I once heard someone pose this question: What is your heroic mission on Earth?

Whoa.

That's a powerful question.

Do we each really have a heroic mission? *Hero* is a word usually reserved for firefighters, paramedics, and police who save lives or for those who die serving their country. *Hero* is also a word too often squandered on guys who win at basketball, baseball, and football.

I was lucky to know a true hero, although he didn't look like one. Strangers driving down our street might have mistaken him for a tired old man. That's what he looked like hunched over in a chair sunning on the porch like a content cat, his dark glasses shading eyes weakened by 96 years and by the terrible things he saw on that beach at Normandy.

No matter how he was feeling, Joe kept his humor, his humanity, and his humility.

The life of Dr. Joseph Foley started out small. His parents were poor Irish immigrants. His dad was a garbage collector in Boston. When Joe's appendix ruptured at 14, a kind doctor left a big imprint on Joe and sparked his interest in medicine. Joe ended up studying neurology.

He had a collection of titles: Emeritus Professor of Neurology, former Chair of the Division of Neurology at Case Western University Medical School, past President of the American Academy of Neurology and of the American Neurological Association. He constantly urged doctors to listen to patients; to keep the patient as the center of their focus, not the disease.

Joe taught doctors to look every patient in the eye and greet every patient by name. One time a woman came to the emergency room complaining of crushing headaches. When no one could find any cause, they sent her to the psych ward. She died before she got there. It turned out she had a brain tumor that had ruptured. No one caught it.

Those who had examined her were beating themselves up for missing the medical diagnosis when Joe pointed out that they missed something else. They neglected to treat her with compassion. He told them that she died without anyone to comfort or console her, without the full measure of compassion that every person deserves.

Joe once went with his former classmates to visit an ill classmate who was in the hospital. The man suffered from depression and had been institutionalized. He was unable or unwilling to communicate. The visitors told endless stories about the good old days for a half hour. Joe made sure they included their sick friend through all of it, even though the man never said a word or responded. He hadn't even opened his eyes during the entire conversation.

When it was time to go, they all stood to leave and each one squeezed the man's hand. Suddenly, he opened his eyes and said, "That was the best half hour I've had in months!"

Joe lived by the words of Winston Churchill: Never, never, never give up. Always communicate with the sickest, weakest person in the room. You never know what hope that person might be able to hear, see, or feel during an examination, conversation, or prayer.

After I mentioned Joe briefly in one of my newspaper columns, a woman from Nashville sent this e-mail:

Dr. Foley was my neurologist many years ago. I vividly remember him. It was the summer of 1968 and I had a grand mal seizure and was hospitalized for a week. I was eight years old and my parents had four other children at home to care for.

Much of the week in the hospital I spent by myself, a very frightening experience for me. Dr. Foley was a gem, kind and caring. Just the kind of doctor an eight-year-old needed. I have his kind face and calm voice imprinted in my brain. He was a big blessing to my eight-year-old self in July 1968.

I spent six years as a pediatric speech-language pathologist before returning to school for my PhD. In my years of clinical work, I worked with many, many children. I realized many years later that my ability to be compassionate and help families as well as children grew from the interactions I had as a child with Dr. Foley and other kind and caring professionals like him.

I sent the e-mail to Joe's family. They read it to him and he laughed.

"There, you see," he said with a grin, "I wasn't all bad."

No, he wasn't. He never even sent the family a bill.

Joe planned to write back to the former patient, but he never regained his strength. That strength was something we thought he'd never lose. He had beaten cancer five times, survived a stroke, a heart valve replacement, and the loss of most of his vision to macular degeneration.

But that scene on the beach never left him. Joe was one of the first doctors to prepare the beach at Normandy before the D-Day invasion. At 28, he was one of the youngest doctors treating the wounded and dying at Licata, Palermo, Termini Imerese, and Normandy. He was with the first unit that went ashore. He ran fast and ducked bullets. He received the Bronze Star and the French Cross for the D-Day invasion. He was able to laugh about that Bronze Star when he told people the citation read: "He exposed himself repeatedly."

Joe talked about how he got off a small boat that morning, waded through the water to get up onto the sand, then ran from machine-gun fire dripping wet. He never forgot the wounded he pulled to safety by the scruff of their necks or the men who perished in the sand or in his arms. He told people that he never saw a dead man without wondering about the parents, wife, or children who would mourn.

When Joe died, hundreds showed up at the funeral, not to mourn but to celebrate the life he lived and all the lives he touched. The Mass was celebrated by six priests and a bishop. My friend Father Don Cozzens gave the eulogy. He said Joe loved attention but saw the danger of being the smartest or funniest person in the room. He knew we are most alive when we die to our ego selves and live for others.

Don said that Joe, like Jacob in the Bible, wrestled with his faith, his God, and his church. He was a coffeehouse theologian who lived those words from Micah 6:8: "Act justly. Love tenderly. Walk humbly with your God."

Near the end of the Mass, these final words were read: "No one is really dead unless they are forgotten." It reminded me of the quote by philosopher William James: "The great use of life is to spend it for something that will outlast it."

That's what we all want. Immortality.

That's what a great life does. It makes you immortal. It lasts long after you are gone. Joe will live on in me, in his patients, in his friends, in his family. In the hospital maintenance worker who called to tell me Dr. Foley always made him feel important. In the countless children of the children of all those he saved on the beaches and in the hospitals.

Joe was married for 59 years, raised six children, and defined his life by love and service. He used to say, "Make sure you love people and behave in a way that you can be loved." That love guided him in everything he did, from the beaches, to the clinics, to the porch, where the man who saw too much war never stopped praying for peace.

Every time I pass by his house and see the empty chair on the porch, I wonder about my own heroic mission in life.

We all have one. And if we find it and do it, we, too, will live forever.

For networking to work, we all have
to be the net.

The huge numbers don't hit you as hard as one single empty chair does.

Or one empty locker.

Or that empty spot at the lunch table.

Empty is how a lot of us have felt riding this economic roller coaster. If you haven't been laid off in the past five years, you know someone who has. We all do.

If you haven't lost your job, you suffer from survivor's guilt when you're among the last ones standing. You want to do something but feel paralyzed.

The *Plain Dealer* newspaper where I work as a columnist lost 27 people in one week to layoffs. It was eerie to pass an empty cubicle where my friend of 22 years sat, a friend who planned to retire as a journalist and suddenly found himself unemployed and unemployable.

We all silently wondered and worried: *Who's next?*

That same week, the Labor Department announced that the unemployment rate had hit 6.7 percent as 533,000 jobs disappeared that November alone, the highest in 34 years.

Like many people, I'm in a business that could one day be obsolete. We keep reading about the demise of newspapers, that our profession is teetering on the edge of oblivion. All across the country, jobs have been slashed at every newspaper. Papers are for sale, in bankruptcy, or have been sold countless times and whittled down to bare bones. Nothing is sacred, not even that sacred trust we call the Fourth Estate. Some papers have folded; some have cut out home delivery; others are publishing online only.

Our business model changed with the Internet. There are no longer enough advertising dollars to cover the bills. The real-estate ads went online, where people can watch a video tour of homes. Employment ads are better online. You can click and submit your résumé. Then there's Craigslist. How do you compete with free? It doesn't matter how great the writing is if there aren't enough advertising dollars to support the paper.

All around me in Cleveland, companies have cut or outsourced jobs. Banks, factories, steel mills, and auto plants have laid off workers by the hundreds. As a columnist, I sometimes joke, "I have the best seat on the *Titanic*." I plan to keep playing until the ship goes down. I hope the newspaper business stays afloat for a long, long time, but every time another paper cuts jobs, I wonder where the lifeboat is.

Who doesn't?

What do you do? Do you jump ship? If so, when?

I think you build a bridge, plank by plank. Then, when the time comes, you have something to walk across. You can build that bridge with others and for others.

That's what we did at the *Plain Dealer*. We couldn't stop the company from cutting jobs, but together we could form a safety net for those who lost their jobs so the landing wouldn't hurt so much. And we could help one another build that bridge.

My husband and I brainstormed an event we called a Media Career Transition Day. It grew into a grassroots effort, with staff in the newsroom providing career help to all those who had lost their jobs. It also prepared the rest of us for that day, should it happen to us.

The purpose was to provide career skills; to focus on the future, not the past. There would be no blaming, no bashing anyone for the situation we were in. The tone was important. We wanted it to be about empowering people for the future.

Our primary audience was the group of 27 employees who were laid off. The secondary audience was any *Plain Dealer* employee interested in acquiring additional career skills. We also wanted to help anyone else in the media facing the same situation.

We decided to make the day free for all those laid off and charge $25 for employees who weren't laid off. Any profits would go to a fund to help those laid off. We set up an online registration so people could pay by credit card or PayPal. We required registration to know how much food to get.

We picked a Saturday in January and found a church willing to donate space for free from 8 a.m. to 3 p.m. Trinity Cathedral in Cleveland had an auditorium, a large kitchen, and breakout rooms. We spent a month setting up the event and recruiting a massive team of volunteers from the community and the *Plain Dealer*. One hundred people registered for the event and 40 presenters volunteered their time. No one received a dime for giving up an entire Saturday to help others.

The night before the event, it started to snow. And snow. And snow. It didn't stop. I worried that no one would show up. What a shock. Nearly everyone did. Some came from hours away, from Toledo, Akron, Elyria, and Columbus. Not only *Plain Dealer* employees, but journalists from surrounding newspapers, the *Beacon Journal*, Elyria *Chronicle*, Toledo *Blade*, *Sun* papers, and the *Cleveland Jewish News*.

People attended who were either laid off or feared they would be and wanted a plan B ready to build a greater career life ahead. We assembled a team of experts to be available all day. They would help people polish their résumés, figure out their next five steps, and find out how to get that second interview.

We gave each participant four tickets to encourage them to talk to at least four different career coaches. They printed their names on the tickets, and each time they met with an expert, they turned in the tickets, which were later pulled for prizes.

The day started with a breakfast of muffins and breads that our coworkers made. A motivational speaker at 9 a.m. got everyone jazzed, then we moved right into a session on résumé writing and how to write cover letters to make journalism skills transferable to other jobs.

The next session was on interviewing skills and how to negotiate a salary and benefits. We also offered a workshop on Internet skills and resources and how to use LinkedIn, Career-

Board, Monster.com, and other sites to find work. During lunch, we had a keynote speaker on networking, informational interviews, and how to make looking for work a full-time job.

The entire afternoon offered a menu of sessions that included the most likely areas in which laid-off journalists would find work: marketing, public relations, advertising, foundations, nonprofits, freelance writing, book publishing, radio, TV, and online work. We had professors, college career placement specialists, and a panel of former newspaper staffers who'd found successful jobs in other fields. Headhunters gave free one-on-one consultations.

We ended the day with a networking reception and desserts provided by our coworkers. We kept reminding everyone, this is *your* day. Make the best use of all the resources here. Don't leave with any regrets. The future is in your hands.

As I watched the room fill with hope, I thought about how my friend Barb used to tell me that life is a series of trapeze bars. You climb 50 feet to the top if you have the nerve, then you stand on the platform, take hold of the bar, and swing out into life. It's exhilarating and the ride is a breeze, until one day you look down and panic. Someone moved the net below. Or there never was one. Or something happens—a downsizing, a layoff, an illness, a divorce, a death—and life starts to pry your fingers off that bar you are holding on to.

It's hard to imagine life sending another opportunity your way as good as the one you have. So you cling tight to the bar you have. You can't see that other bar coming at you, or if you can, it's out of reach. And that's the scary part.

To grab on to the next bar, you have to let go of the one

you're holding on to. Once you do—you are in midair hanging on to absolutely nothing.

I looked around the room and saw people relax their grip on that bar and get excited as they explored what the next one might look like. At the end of the day, many were in tears as they thanked us for giving them hope.

Instead of dreading the unknown, they were looking forward to soaring toward it. They were ready to let go of who they used to be to discover who they could become.

If you don't want regrets at the end of your life, have no regrets at the end of each day.

The frail, white-haired woman came into my life more than a decade ago for only five minutes. It was summer and a friend introduced the two of us. Her name was Olga, and I never saw her again. It could have been one of those thousands of brief introductions that are usually forgotten five minutes later.

Olga looked like an 80-year-old but had the energy of a 3-year-old. When she heard I was going on vacation, she was as excited as if she were going. She told me there were two rules for vacation and that if you follow them, you'll have a great time no matter where you travel:

Rule 1: Speak up about what you want to do and do it.
Rule 2: Don't have any regrets at the end of any day.

Good rules for vacation.

Great rules for life.

It made me wonder why we save our best living for vacation and spend the other weeks waiting, whining, and pining for the chance to live the way we really want to.

Rule 1 sounds easy, but too often we make people guess at what we want, so of course, we don't usually get it. Not just on special days like vacations, birthdays, and holidays, but on normal days, like Tuesday. We've all done it. You're in the mood for Italian food and your husband says, "Honey, what do you want to eat tonight?" You answer, "I don't care," and you get stuck eating Chinese. You want to watch a football game and your wife asks, "Honey, what do you want to do?" You answer, "It's up to you," and you end up getting stuck shopping for curtains.

If you speak up, there's a risk you may not get what you want. But if you don't speak up, you're pretty much guaranteed not to get it.

As for Rule 2, it's up to us to live a life free of regrets. We can blame our jobs, our bosses, our spouses, our parents, our children, or our genetic material for our limitations, but in the end, our lives are what we choose to make them.

Annie Dillard once wrote that how you spend your days is ultimately how you spent your life. That one line stopped me cold. It was like a death sentence. Or a life sentence. Was how I spent my days really how I would spend my life? Wow. It sounded terrible, until I changed how I spent my days.

I spent a lot of days whining about what I didn't have time to do, lamenting over what I wished I could do if only... What was I waiting for?

If it's true that how we spend our days is how we spend our lives, most obituaries aren't honest. They never say that Jane Doe spent her life eating bonbons and watching *One Life to Live*. But if that is how she spent her days, isn't that indeed how she spent her life?

How about John Doe, who spends his days at a job he hates and the rest of the time sitting on a barstool complaining about it? It may seem to him like one day wasted, but in the end, it's a life wasted. His obit will list the children he had, even the ones that stopped speaking to him years ago. It will list the grandchildren, even if he hadn't seen them in four years and never even knew their names.

I once read that you should write out your own obituary— the way you would want it to read—to find out what your real desires are. Try it. Spend an hour of your vacation or weekend or lunch hour writing down how you would have wanted to live. It could jump-start your new life.

I do two things that keep me from having regrets. After watching a video of Steve Jobs give a commencement address to Stanford University, I wrote down the question he asked himself every day. His words are on a card that I read every morning. When I open the medicine chest to get my toothbrush, there it is: "If today were the last day of my life, would I want to do what I'm about to do today?" Then I pause and make sure the answer is yes. If the answer is no, I rethink my day.

Then, at the end of the day, I practice the tenth step of Alcoholics Anonymous that my friends in recovery taught me: "Continued to take personal inventory, and when we were wrong, promptly admitted it." They taught me to do a quick scan of the day before bed to see if I closed my heart to anyone by being selfish, dishonest, unfair, resentful, fearful, or angry. Was I kind and compassionate? Did I think of others or just myself? Was there anyone I hurt? Anyone I need to apologize to? It's just a quick scan, not a flogging. Then I ask God to bless anyone I hurt by my action or inaction, and I pray for the grace to make amends the next day.

Do it long enough, and you right your wrongs just before you veer off course. You catch yourself, apologize, correct your course, and move on. You don't drag any hostages to bed with you or wake up with them and drag them into the next day. Everyone is free. No more emotional hangovers.

Daily self-appraisal keeps you in check so your whole life doesn't get off course. Some people do a quick inventory during the day as soon as they feel something go haywire. You pause, step back, and examine your thoughts, feelings, and actions, not the other person's.

I don't want to get to the end of my life and be buried under regrets. Too many people do. Hospice workers have shared with me the regrets they hear from people in the last months of their lives: They were too scared to live the lives they truly wanted to live. They failed to make amends with siblings, parents, spouses, children. They worked too much and wished they could have those precious hours back. They worried too much about small details that didn't matter. They wished they had said "I love you" more and "I told you so" less. They lost touch with dear friends and let them slip away. They never figured out how to be happy with life on life's terms.

My friend Sarah Maxwell used to work as a music therapist at Hospice of the Western Reserve in Cleveland. She helped people make peace with the past, helped them mend relationships before they left this world. One day Sarah asked if I could do one of her patients a favor. One woman wanted me to share her last regret. Mrs. R. was 80 and wrote this dying message:

As I lie in bed, numerous volunteers have brightened my days. As I see the joy that they give and receive, I have feelings of regret. I lived down the street from a nursing home and I never thought about giving of my time and going there to bring a smile to a lonely person's face. I will feel that I made a difference if I am able to convince others to give even one hour a week in volunteering. You can be a hospice volunteer or a visitor to a nursing home or a tutor in a school. There are so many good people doing good things. Be one of them.

That was her dying wish. Give one hour of time a week so you don't end up dying with the same regret.

At the end of life, what will be your one regret?

What is in the gap between the life you are living and the life you want to be living? Once you know it, you can start living the life you want to be living, the only one worth living.

Find your grail. Be who God meant you to be, and you will set the world on fire.

Every spring the parents start to panic.

As college seniors prepare to graduate, their loved ones call and write me for advice: *My daughter, [my son,] is graduating from college and there are no jobs. They spent all that time and money to prepare for a career that might not exist. What can I say or do to give them hope?*

Before you start making room in your basement for them to move in, give them the greatest graduation gift there is: believe in them.

Hope for the next generation isn't found in the want ads. You make your own hope. No job I ever had in my life was found in the want ads or online. They all came to me by aligning myself on the inside first and connecting with the right people already in my life. They all came to me when I looked past the unemployment rate and remembered that God is always hiring.

Don't believe the rejection letters. Believe beyond the statistics. Believe in spite of the facts. Believe in your place in this world even when the world doesn't believe in you.

You have to believe in yourself even when no one else does. You have to believe bigger than the disbelief around you. You have to believe in miracles, in what you can't see.

That might mean you have to create the job you want. You might have to design the life you want to live. Three years ago, I made a fake book cover and wrote my name down as the author. It inspired me to buckle down and write my first book. My real book is now on sale at bookstores near you.

Before I finished writing my first book, I printed out the *New York Times* best seller list and taped it to my office door. I boldly put the title of my own book on it. My first book made the real *New York Times* best seller list three weeks in a row.

My vision board has a photo of me chatting with Oprah. Okay, so I cut off Sally Field's head (sorry, I really do like you, Sally) and put mine there. Why not dream big?

You have to design the life you want to have. Name it, claim it, and start living it.

Stop telling yourself, *I don't know what to do.* You know something. Start with what you know. Ask yourself, *What do I know for sure?* Start there.

I used to tell myself, *I'm scared,* all the time, so I attracted more fear. A big wad of it, like those giant rubber-band balls. That was me. Layer upon layer, that ball of fear grew. No more. I told myself, *Snap out of it. Go make something possible.*

I'll never forget the first time I heard the students from the Baldwin Wallace University music theatre program sing their hearts out at Nighttown in Cleveland Heights. They blew me away. They're all on their way to Broadway. Talk about a dream out of reach. The odds are against them. They don't care. Their joy was so contagious, my face hurt from smiling as they belted out these lyrics from a *Spamalot* song: "If you trust in your song, keep your eyes on the goal, then the prize you won't fail, that's your grail. So be strong, keep right on, to the end of your song. Do not fail. Find your grail."

The Holy Grail might be mythical, but a holy grail is what we each are, a sacred container for the holy, for God. Saint Catherine of Siena said, "Be who God meant you to be and you will set the world on fire."

You can tell when someone does that. Jeffery Zaslow did it. He was a vessel for the holy. You knew him through all the books he wrote. Jeff gave voice to Randy Pausch in *The Last Lecture*. He gave Gabby Giffords words to tell her story. He gave Captain Sully more than a moment on the Hudson in a plane in the water. He gave the girls from Ames a chance to share their friendship and inspire that same love for others all over the world.

I met Jeff in 2000 when he won the Will Rogers Humanitarian Award from the National Society of Newspaper Columnists. I was once president of the NSNC, a fun-loving bunch of columnists from all over the country. Jeff was chosen for the award because he did so much to spotlight good, decent people doing good, decent things for the world.

That's what Jeff always was: a good, decent human being. He looked out for others. He looked for the good in others. He captured it and disappeared in the process. He let others shine through his words. Trappist monk Thomas Merton once wrote, "Let me at least disappear into the writing I do...The work could be a prayer."

Jeff's life truly was a prayer. A prayer for others.

He used to write a column in Chicago called "All that Zazz" and held an annual Zazz Bash for singles. Thousands attended. He helped 78 couples find their soul mates to marry.

Jeff was writing columns for the *Wall Street Journal* the year he heard the last lecture by Randy Pausch, a computer science professor at Carnegie Mellon University in Pittsburgh. Randy had pancreatic cancer. Half of those diagnosed die within six months. The odds of surviving an airliner crash are 24 percent; the odds of surviving pancreatic cancer are 4 percent.

He had mere months to live when Jeff shared his story with the world. Randy died on July 25, 2008, at 47. He left behind a wife and three kids, ages 6, 3, and 2. I watched the last lecture online and cried at the end. The day he gave his last lecture was also his wife's birthday, the last one they would ever celebrate together. When they wheeled out a giant cake, she rushed onstage, threw her arms around him, and whispered in his ear: "Please don't die. The magic will go out of our lives."

I don't know if the magic went out of their lives. I do know the magic went into our lives, thanks to Jeff. The book has been translated into 48 languages and millions have watched that last lecture online and are busy climbing walls instead of being stopped by them. Jeff gave us a foot up to climb ours.

"Go hug your kids," he said. "Go love your life."

The last time he was in Cleveland, we talked before and after his book event. He said traveling was brutal and he couldn't wait to get home to his wife and children.

I still can't believe that he died in a car accident on his way home from a book signing one snowy day in February 2012. He was 53.

Jeff helped me many times when I was stuck. We chatted on the phone or by e-mail, and he was never too busy to return a call or urge me on into the amazing world of authordom that he inhabited with such humility and grace. He even gave me a blurb for my first book, *God Never Blinks*, which I treasure now more than ever.

He still inspires me every day. I keep his business card next to my computer where I write: *Jeffrey Zaslow, Senior Special Writer, The Wall Street Journal*. It's next to one of the quotes by Randy Pausch: "Inspiration is the ultimate tool for doing good."

Jeff once told me after a book signing that he was tired of being on the road, that he just wanted to hug his kids and kiss his wife. His last book was inspired by his love for his three daughters: *The Magic Room: A Story about the Love We Wish for Our Daughters*.

The Magic Room.

I imagine he is in one now, interviewing everyone there, fascinated by every story.

Acknowledgments

There is no way to thank everyone who makes a book possible, especially a book about work. Countless bosses and coworkers shaped the person I am. It's impossible to list them all, but I am grateful for their fingerprints all over my life.

My first and greatest teacher about work was my dad, Tom Brett. He worked harder than any human being should work. He instilled in all 11 children a work ethic stronger than steel. My mom, Mary Brett, worked harder than any mother should, changing diapers, cooking meals, washing mountains of laundry day after day, year after year. I owe them both a debt of gratitude that can never be repaid.

I also want to thank...

My siblings, in-laws, and their children for loving me more than I deserve.

All my teachers at Immaculate Conception Elementary

Acknowledgments

School, Brown Junior High School, Ravenna High School, Kent State University, and John Carroll University for opening my mind and filling it with wonder.

All the people who hired me over the years at jobs great and small and gave me the chance to meet so many wonderful colleagues who taught me so many of these life lessons.

The loyal readers who read my columns, attend my talks, buy my books, send e-mails, and trust me to tell their stories. Thanks for sharing your experiences, strengths, and hopes.

My Polish publishers, Tomasz, Maria, and Pawel Brzozowski at Insignis Media, and the many readers in Poland who made me a best-selling author in their lovely country. Dziekuje! A special thanks to Dominika Pycińska for making my trip there a joy and a blessing.

The many writers whose love and support have lifted me for decades, including Sheryl Harris, Thrity Umrigar, Bill O'Connor, Dick Feagler, Ted Gup, Susan Ager, and Stuart Warner.

Two great mentors who left this world too soon, Gary Blonston and Jeffrey Zaslow.

Minister Joyce Meyer, whose tweet inspired the title of this book.

The *Plain Dealer* and the *Beacon Journal* for giving me the freedom to do my best work and for granting me permission to share it in this book.

My agent, Linda Loewenthal at David Black Literary Agency, for her great wisdom, laser clarity, and gentle honesty that guide me like a compass.

My team at Grand Central Publishing: Publisher Jamie Raab for believing in me and my writing with such zeal and exuberance. Editor Karen Murgolo, whose kindness and passion make the editing process pure pleasure. Matthew Ballast and Nicole Bond, for spreading my writing all over the world. And to everyone else there who put their mark on this book.

My front-row friends, especially Beth Welch, Kay Peterson, Vicki Prussak, Sheryl Harris, Katie O'Toole, Suellen Saunders, and Sharon Sullivan.

To the joy of my life, my grandchildren, Asher, Ainsley, and River, who remind me to play hard and savor every morsel of fun in each moment by staying completely present in it.

To my children, Gabrielle, James, Ben, and Joe, for living such interesting, joyful lives that constantly open my mind and heart to new wonders.

To my husband, Bruce, who believed in me long before I did and absolutely cherishes me and celebrates everything life has given us.

And, as always, endless gratitude to the Source of it all, the God of my joy.

About the Author

Regina Brett is the *New York Times* best-selling author of *God Never Blinks: 50 Lessons for Life's Little Detours* and *Be the Miracle: 50 Lessons for Making the Impossible Possible.* Her writing has been translated into numerous languages and published in more than 26 countries.

Her famous 50 Life Lessons have traveled the world, but contrary to the popular Internet rumor, Regina is not 90.

Regina also writes columns for the *Plain Dealer* in Cleveland and for the *Cleveland Jewish News* and is syndicated through the Jewish News Service. Regina has twice been named a finalist for the Pulitzer Prize in Commentary.

Regina lives in Cleveland, Ohio, with her husband, Bruce.

She welcomes readers to visit her at www.reginabrett.com and to follow her on Facebook at ReginaBrettFans and on Twitter at @reginabrett.